REMAIN

ROB LINK

Other books by Rob Link
Pulse: You Can't Heal What You Can't Feel

Rascals: Weird, Wacky, and Wonderful Stories from an Inner City Church

The King of Rascals

Become

Introduction

"Remain in me and you will bear much fruit," Jesus said.

Hmm.

Sounds easy enough.

If we want to bear fruit, be impactful, live lives of significance all we need do is remain.

Sounds easy enough.

But it isn't.

In fact "being still and knowing He is God," (Ps. 46:10) is one of the hardest things we will ever do. We are a busy people living in a busy world. Taking time to sit in the presence of the Lord and reflect on Him, His thoughts, and His plans for us is almost impossible.

To make a regular habit of getting alone with the savior takes a herculean effort on our parts.

But it is worth it.

It is worth the effort.

This little book is my stab at making it a bit easier for you to sit before the Lord. I've written several short devotionals for you in hope that they draw you a bit closer to the King.

I have asked several of my friends to contribute with a daily devotion for you to read and reflect upon. I'm very thankful for their labor (as you will be too, once you've read their offerings).

Inside you will find over 100 readings, varying in length – all easy to read. I've included some questions to ponder after each entry. Use them if they are helpful. Ignore them if they aren't.

As I compiled these short reflections I envisioned them being used in a couple ways.

1. As a devotional to be read alone during the daily time set aside for the Lord.

2. After dinner, around the table, with the family and/or friends.

Whether or not you use this book in either of these two

ways or in a way unique to you – it doesn't matter. I simply hope you use it and find it helpful in your efforts to remain close to the Father, the Son, and the Spirit.

Peace and Joy,
Rob

Slow Down
by Rob Link

Slow down.

Just slow down.

You know it's been said if the devil can't make you bad he'll just make you busy. Hmmm... I think there is truth to that. Busy–ness is one of America's greatest problems. We are always rushing from this to that. We are hurrying from here to there. Hurry, hurry, hurry.

There is a reason the Lord gave his people the Sabbath. There is a reason the Word says to "be still." The reason is that when we are always on the go, we eventually wind up running on empty. And when we run on empty we run into trouble of all kinds.

So slow down.

Slow down.

Just slow down.

Silence is Golden
by Rob Link

Sometimes it is best to say nothing.

When a friend is grieving – just sit there, don't say anything.

When someone is irrational with anger – don't say anything, they won't listen no matter how wise your words are.

When you do not have an answer – no need to pretend. Just shut your mouth and don't say anything.

There are times when the situation simply calls for silence.

Do you know someone who talks too much?

Has it ever been said about you that you talk too much?

Here's your homework: talk less this week.

Unplug
by Dori Beltz

The #1 misplaced or broken item in our house is definitely headphones.

Or ear buds. Or whatever they're called.

Anyway, they're a hot commodity. So many devices, so few headphones.

I've lost track of how many times each day I get through 90 seconds of highly valuable information before someone says, "Are you talking to me?"

Ugh.

"Listen, my son, and be wise, and set your heart on the right path."

(Proverbs 23:19) I love the Book of Proverbs.

Winsome, yet weighty. Chocked full of practical advice on how to be your best for God and for others. Like this one…gently prodding people to pull the noise out of their ears and listen.

To listen = wisdom. So that must mean that not listening, "tuning out", or inserting small wire-and-foam distraction-delivering gadgets brings about foolishness.

Ain't that the truth.

How many times has a parent or friend said emphatically, "Are you listening to me?"

It's not an NFL problem
by Rob Link

The NFL, which rakes in somewhere between $9-$10 billion dollars (yes, that's Billion with a B) each year, has had some incredibly bad press.

To say that that bad press is deserved would be a massive understatement. The bad press has been more than warranted.

Within a particular two-week period there was a video-proven case of domestic violence, two more cases of domestic violence, and a case of horrible child abuse.

The justified outcry against the NFL was loud and came from every place imaginable.

Yet in spite of all of this I don't think the NFL has a problem.

I'll say that again to make sure you get it. I don't think the NFL has a problem.

I think America has a problem.

To simply name these issues as NFL issues would be an act of both injustice and ignorance.

Most research agrees that 1 in 4 or 1 in 5 women will be a victim of domestic violence at least once in their life. For children it is shown to be 1 in 10 with many experts commenting that it is a bit lower because the child's mom will often step in between the child and the abuser and receives the abuse that was headed the child's way.

This isn't an NFL problem.

It's bigger than that.
It's a national problem that has exhibited itself in the NFL.

I suppose there are many steps/actions/forums/discussions that can help alleviate this awful reality of our country.

I want to bring up one, and I'll bring it up with a few questions.

Where are all the strong yet gentle men who will strongly stand against this garbage while walking gently with people – women, children, and men?

Where's the voice of male kindness that speaks its own

type of strength?

Where are all the godly men – godly in the sense that they are more than willing to put themselves last for the sake of others?

Where are all the non-passive men who refuse to let other men use their strength for harm?

Maybe that one deserves a second take so here it is: where are all the non-passive men?

Where are the men who realize being physically stronger doesn't mean winning any and every disagreement?

Maybe I could ask all that simply this way:

Where are the men?

The way of violence and abuse is not the way of a man.

Where are the men?

I think I know where they are.

They are in countless homes, churches, synagogues, neighborhoods, and schools. They are in the grocery store and at the gas station. They are in New York and LA. They are in Alaska and Hawaii. They are found in every possible demographic – age, race, education, and socio economic status.

They are everywhere.

Even in the NFL.

In fact it is my belief that the good guys are far more plentiful than the bad guys.

But I think they are scared. Fearful. Frozen in passivity. Overwhelmed. Fraught with insecurities and doubt.

I want you to wonder with me. I want you to imagine.

What if all those scared, fearful, passive, overwhelmed, insecure and doubt filled men stood up in the midst of all those fears? What if us men would fetch a batch of courage and act in spite of the fear? What if all the good guys decided that standing for that which is right is more important than sitting for fear? What if we lived like Jesus, which means dying for others? What if...

I wonder.

What if?

If you are "one of the good guys," say no to passivity! What would that look like for you?

If you are a woman, pray for the "good guys" to stand up. Who will you be praying for?

Fear
by Jared Caron

Is fear a lack of faith?

When I live in fear I begin to let the enemy in. I think to myself that I just need to pray more or stay focused. I need to fight harder for my faith.

I believe now that fear is faith in the wrong way.

Fear is not the absence of faith. It is faith in the wrong thing.

Fear is faith that things (whatever it might be) are bigger than God's ability to handle them.

The devil (yes he does exist) has fooled us into that way of living.

I mean what person do you know who does not struggle with fear, fear of failure, fear of money, fear of body image and the list goes on and on!

If you live more in fear then you do in Faith your fear

muscle will get stronger and your faith muscle gets weaker, taking you farther from God and closer to the devil.

I say we fight back by walking into the unknown with the power of the cross and the truth that Jesus gives us!

The truth is that if we follow Jesus with all our hearts then we have nothing to Fear!

How strong is your fear muscle?

How strong is your fear muscle?

When that fear comes in, bring the cross in to the middle of it, push back and walk in TRUTH not Lies!

I was mad
by Rob Link

I was mad in a meeting.

Really mad.

And disappointed.

But mostly mad.

I knew without question that I needed to stand and speak my mind to all the folks in the room. They would hear my anger as I vented. I didn't care if my angry venting did damage. I was mad.

And then…

And then that still small voice of the Lord whispered in my head,

"Would you rather be angry or influential?"

"Would you rather vent or have impact?"

Two small questions and I was convicted to the core. I didn't vent. I spoke kindly and gently.

No one saw my anger, because it had dissipated.

Looking at the damage I almost unleashed, I had this thought,

"Whew, that was a close one. Thank you Jesus."

When was the last time your venting did harm?

To whom do you need to apologize?

Would you rather vent or have influence? Be honest. Look at your actions. They will answer this question for you.

The Secret Place
by Rob Link

Some old dead (and wise) guy once said there are 3 types of truth about the self.

1. There is the public truth about ourselves that we readily and willingly convey to others. i.e. I have kids, I'm married, I work at…
2. There is the private truth about ourselves that we only let ourselves know. i.e. I am scared of mice, I don't like so and so…
3. And lastly, there is the truth about ourselves that we don't even know (or maybe it's the truth about ourselves we don't let ourselves know). Only God knows this type of truth.

It is at that 3rd level where the action is.

The guy who works out all the time might be doing so because deep down and unknowingly he feels fat, unmanly, ugly. So he lives at the gym.

The woman who is a workaholic might be doing so because some place in her subconscious – unbeknownst to her – the voice from that old teacher echoes, "you'll never amount to anything!" So she overworks.

The husband who is continually distant and unengaged might be doing so because deep within he is haunted with an unknown belief that he will never have what it takes to be a good husband. So he withdraws.

It's this 3rd level of truth that dictates many of our actions and beliefs.

The bummer of this 3rd level of truth is that the "truth" we believe deep down, unknowingly, is often not even true.

It's often a lie.

That guy isn't fat and ugly. That woman will and has amounted to something. And that husband does have what it takes.

I'll say it again; it's this 3rd level of truth that dictates many of our actions and beliefs.

And it is at this 3rd level where God likes to do his work in us.

"You will know the truth, and the truth will set you free," says the Bible.

Note it isn't the truth alone that sets you free. It is the truth you know that will set you free.

If you are brave enough.

If you are patient enough to be still.

God will take you to the 3rd level and speak his truth to the deep and secret places.

And therein lies freedom.

What is the "public" truth about you?

What is the "private" truth about you?

If you had to guess, what is that "3rd level" truth about you?

Take some time, to sit with the Lord and ask him about that 3rd level truth.

Halt Deer
by Rob Link

It's been said, "if you have a pulse, you've got issues."

So true.

Sometimes those issues can get the best of us.

Bummer.

Here's what I've learned when it comes to my issues: HALT

Hurt. Angry. Lonely. Tired.

HALT.

When HALT happens I am more susceptible to letting my issues get the best of me.

So are you.

So beware. This is helpful. If we know when we are more prone to stumble maybe we will be less prone to stumble during those times when we are more prone to stumble. (Read that brain-twisting sentence again.)

DEER.

DEER is helpful. When DEER happens I am less likely to have my issues trip me up. You could say that when HALT happens (or is happening) I'm best off if I get me some DEER.

Devotions. Exercise. Eating. Rest.

These things keep me healthy mentally and spiritually.

When I say devotions I'm not talking about some boring, impersonal, religious thing. Rather I'm talking about that rich and meaningful time with God that everyone has experienced at least once. (Maybe it was that moving Christmas Eve service when you were a kid or that time you really felt God's presence on vacation in the mountains...) When I'm engaged in this daily, life is sweeter.

It will be for you too.

Devotions. Regularly.

Exercise. When we move as humans (as opposed to going the way of the couch potato) good things happen. Scientists will talk about endorphins and such. I don't know much about that. I do know however that when I am in a good rhythm and routine in regard to exercise I simply feel better.

You will too.

Exercise. Regularly.

I love pizza. I love lasagna. I love them so much that I can single handedly east enough of these ambrosiatic foods to feed an army. Yet the truth is, I always feel kinda icky when I overeat. Although it is more difficult to eat well, balanced, and moderately, I feel freer and more alive when I do the harder thing.

You will too.

Eat. Healthily.

Here's a fact: sleepy people are grumpy people. Here's another fact: rest is good. Here's a third fact: God rested on day 7 (to model what is good and right for us silly humans). So get some sleep. Take a nap. Go to bed a bit earlier. Or sleep in a bit later. Do less. Rest more. When I am rested I am a better person for all those around me.

Rest. Regularly.

Beware the HALT.

Embrace the DEER.

When are you most likely to stumble?

What would it take for you to start DEER in your life?

Self-Denial
by Brian Fraaza

Self-denial is self-improvement.

That means that by not getting to do or have everything that you want, you are actually growing in your character. It makes you more like Jesus.

As sinful people, we tend to think about ourselves first most of the time which can cause us to put what we want in the moment (I want this RIGHT NOW!) ahead of what we know is best.

I do it with everything, from food (I want a large pizza) to television (I want to watch the game) to exercise (I DON'T want to exercise today) and tons of other things I can't even think of right now.

Now none of these things are bad by themselves. They can all be good in moderation...but I'm not good at moderation. There is something good that happens when we deny ourselves something on purpose. It's a sort of calm and clarity that comes over the brain. Everything else in life slows down a bit and we begin to see things more clearly.

When I am in this zone, it's much easier to hear God talking. What he usually says to me during one of these times is about trading something good (a large pizza or a video game) for something much better (the peace and contentment of resting with God).

I think this is why Jesus instructed his disciples to fast (stop eating food for a short time).

> *"When you fast, do not look somber as the hypocrites do, for they disfigure their faces to show others they are fasting. Truly I tell you, they have received their reward in full."*
> *Matthew 6:16*

He knew that by giving something up, life would slow down a bit and they would re-focus their energies on the things that matter and let the stuff that wasn't important slide away. Self-denial is self-improvement.

When you pray today, ask God if there is anything he would like you to give up for a day or two. What did he say?

Try it, and spend a few extra minutes talking with God. See what happens.

Bad Tattoos
by Rob Link

I was playing around the other night on twitter. I came across a rather interesting site.

Bad tattoos.

It had pictures. Lots of pictures.

Oh my.

I think I woke Kristy with my loud laughs.

Some of the pictures where just plain funny.

All of them were appalling.

After laughing I began to think, "what were these people thinking!?"

Upon further review I could see that many of the people who had the bad tattoos were thinking, "what was I thinking!?"

To be sure you can get a bad tattoo removed, but it's going to leave a mark. The skin is disfigured permanently. Either with the bad tattoo or the ensuing scars that come with the effort to remove it.

A lot of people think their bad choices (i.e. sins) are like bad tattoos.

They leave you marred forever. Oh sure you might work hard to remove the sin, but the scars remain.

And many think this is how the God of the Bible views us sinful critters.

Stained or scarred.

Or worse.

Both.

But I want to tell you something. So you better listen. Open your ears to hear while your eyes take in these words.

The God revealed in the Bible does not hold our poor choices and sin against us! He does not see us as marred forever because of our stupid mistakes!

In fact the opposite is true!

(I realize I just finished the last 3 sentences with exclamation marks and thus am at risk of being compared to a middle school girl. But I am excited about the truths those sentences contain!! So I don't care!!!)

The Bible says, "if anyone is in Christ they are a new creation. The old is gone. See everything is new."

Now that's good news. Well actually that is great news! (OK, no more exclamation marks.)

That is great news to everyone who has ever made a dumb mistake.

It is great news to everyone who has every made a poor choice.

It's great news to everyone who has felt like Hester Prynne – that lady from *The Scarlet Letter* – forever marked and labeled by their sin and short comings.

It's great news for everybody who has ever failed, dropped the ball, hurt somebody, screwed up, messed up, been stupid, made a mistake, made a lifetime of mistakes…

The cross and empty tomb took care of all that.

It's great news.

If anyone (yes including you) is in Christ they are a new creation. The old is gone. Everything is new.

Here's your homework:

Get to know Jesus.

And since he doesn't hold your sin against you, you stop holding your sin against you.

Are you able to embrace the truth that God doesn't hold your sinfulness against you?

What things (i.e. thoughts or actions) are you holding against yourself?

Let those things go. Let yourself off the hook. If necessary see a therapist or tell a friend. Whatever you need to do to enable yourself to let it go – do it.

Be Happy
by Todd Kingma

Several years ago radio stations were constantly playing a song that had caught everyone's attention. Most people didn't know most of the song's words, but they did sing the song's title – "Don't Worry, Be Happy" – over and over. It did not matter where you were or what you were doing. You could not escape hearing those words, "Don't worry, be happy".

Over time, of course, people became tired of the song and moved on. New songs became popular. And today, it's hard to find anyone who sings "Don't Worry, Be Happy" anymore.

I mention this old song because it offers a good lesson for all of us.

You see, it's easy to sing "Don't worry, be happy", but that does not really make anyone truly happy. That's why most people chase things like clothes, computers, phones, cars, sports, alcohol, sex…whatever. But over time, just like the song, we get tired of those things and need to move on to other things that will hopefully "make us happy." Sadly, most people today never really find out what can make them happy.

So where do you go to find out how to "be happy"? I recommend that you take a look at what the Bible has to say about being happy. I bet you will be surprised to see that the Bible actually has a lot of good suggestions. Here are just a few.

Happy are those who…
- study God's law (James 1:25)
- are kind to the needy (Proverbs 14:21)
- plan peace (Proverbs 12:20)
- respect the Lord and have their hope in the Lord (Psalm 146:5)
- live pure lives, follow the Lord's teachings, keep his rules, and obey him with their whole heart (Psalm 119:1-2)
- are humble, want to do right, show mercy, have pure thinking and work to bring peace (Matthew 5:3-9)
- listen to wisdom (Proverbs 8:34)
- trust the Lord and do not turn to those who are proud or worship false gods (Psalm 40:4)
- do not listen to the wicked, go where sinners go, or do what evil people do (Psalm 1:1-2)

I cannot promise you that if you do all of this that your life will be easy or that you will be an instant success. That's not what is promised. But I can assure you that, if you do these things, you will definitely be happy.

Trust me on this one.

Make it a habit to follow the Bible's advice from the passages noted above. And if you do, I know that you really will be happy.

What are you doing during those times you are the happiest?

Is your happiness tied to how other people view you? Or on whether you meet someone else's expectations for you? If so, is this good? Does it make you really happy?

Take another look at how the Bible describes happy people. What surprises you about that list? How much of it do you actually do in your day-to-day activities? Could you do more?

Do you hang around with people that help make you happy or take away your happiness?

No Favorites
by Rob Link

My boys and I had a chat the other day (Jake, Max, and Zeke). I had herd the older boys joking around with Zeke saying he is "dad's favorite."

I had to set 'em straight on a couple things.

Firstly – I have no favorites when it comes to my boys (or the girls for that matter, we have two). There is an overwhelming sense of love and enjoyment that I feel for each of Kristy's and my 5 kids.

Secondly – I totally see how the older two could have drawn that conclusion. Why? Because I spend more time with Zeke than I do with Jake or Max.

Not my choice. Theirs.

Zeke chooses to spend time with me a majority of the time when the opportunity presents itself.

Jake and Max don't.

Understandably and even naturally the older two are busier with extracurricular activities. Zeke hasn't yet entered the arena of school sports.

But that isn't the only thing that shortens their time with their dear old dad.

When they have free time, they choose more often than not to hang with their friends. Nothing wrong with that. They have some great friends.

Yet, the down side is they have less time to be with me. Which means they don't get the benefit of being in my presence.

Sounds a bit pretentious to say that simply being in my presence has benefit.

But it is true.

When the boys (and the girls) hang with me they get to encounter things that they wouldn't other wise. Blessings if you will. Trips to the movie's, a visit to Circle K for a 73 cent polar pop, dog park with Barkly, talking and processing school, singing along to 80's metal (OK so this one is debatable as to whether or not it is a benefit), and generally growing deeper intimacy in our father/child relationship.

I see a parallel.

Jesus revealed God as Abba when he taught his disciples to pray.

Abba.

Aramaic for dad.

Daddy.

Like me with my kids, Abba shows no favoritism.

None what-so-ever.

Yet it appears that way, as some seem to receive more divine blessings than others.

Here's why that is: some people choose to spend time with Abba while others don't.

There are benefits and blessings that come along with getting in The Fathers presence.

Those benefits and blessings are for all who would choose to spend time with Him.

I recommend you get yourself some of those benefits.

How much time did or do you spend with your dad (earthly father)?

How much time do you spend with Abba (heavenly dad)?

What keeps you from taking some time each day to be with Abba?

Generous

by Wil Crooks

Can you eat something right now if you wanted to? Do you have a bed to sleep on? Do you have a bike, pair of shoes, more than one change of clothes? Do you go to school? Do you have some cash in your room? If you answered yes to these questions, do you know what that makes you? It makes you very, very rich!

Millions of children around the world don't know where their next meal is coming from. They can't afford to go to school. They sleep on the ground and are lucky to own a pair of worn out shoes. Many children walk long distances just to get clean water to drink, cook with, and to wash their bodies.

It's pretty crazy to think we have all this stuff in our homes when so many people all over the world are struggling just to put food in their stomachs, drink clean water, clothe themselves, and buy a pencil so they can go to school.

If you had a friend at school that didn't have a pencil or didn't have lunch to eat, what would you do? Of course, you would give him one of your extra pencils or share your lunch. That's the Jesus in you. John the Baptist said in the book of Luke, "If you have extra clothes, share with the person who needs clothes and if you have extra food – do the same."

Generosity means to openly share what God has given to you. A great way to live for God is to see your possessions as a way to bless others in need.

Memorize:
> *The generous will themselves be blessed, for they share their food with the poor.*
> *Proverbs 22:9*

Have you ever thought about giving some of your clothes or shoes away to the poor?

Could you make this a project for your family?

Would you consider having your family sponsor a child and you build a relationship with an orphan that lives in a poor country? One organization for you to consider is Children's HopeChest (www.hopechest.org).

Friends
by Rob Link

You might have read the devotional titled "Bad Tattoos." It was originally a blog post. When I wrote it, I thought it was good and was excited to get it out into the blogosphere. Too be honest what I was most excited about was sharing some visual examples of bad tattoos. There were two in particular that made me laugh out loud. They were clearly in bad taste (that's what made them funny) yet I felt like they weren't too inappropriate to share.

I was a bit shocked when everyone at work saw them and said there is no way we could post them on The River website.

Everyone.

Unanimous.

Yet they all laughed.

And they still had no doubt. We were not going to use the pictures I chose.

I was mildly disappointed yet acquiesced none-the-less. The replacement pictures of bad tattoos were much more tame.

Since then I have shown the two pictures to several people. Two things have become apparent.

1. The pictures are funny.

2. There is no way they should be used on our web site.

Turns out my friends at church saved me from crossing a line I shouldn't cross.

Thanks friends.

I think this is why God said that it wasn't good for Adam to be alone. Or in another place "Two are better than one." I was reminded with my poor choice photos that we were meant to live in community.

Friends make us better.

Who is in your circle of friends?

When was the last time they "saved" you from a bad choice?

How often do you spend time with these friends?

Friends 2
by Rob Link

I ran a marathon once.

The training about killed me.

Yet I'm glad I did it. I'll do another one some day.

I hiked the entire length of Isle Royle once by myself in two and a half days. Man, was that work. Yet I'd do it again.

One summer I learned how to read Greek. It was tough and time consuming. But it was cool.

My dog is very well trained. Highly obedient. It took 2 hours a day for the first 6 months of his slobbery life. There is no doubt all those hours were well spent.

And...

And...

And I have a life rich with community and deep friendships.

Getting to this place was harder work than training for a marathon, hiking Isle Royle, learning Greek and training a dog.

It took work.

Hard work.

The last devo was about friends and their value. In this devotional, I want to tell you that deep and lasting friendship does not come easy.

By nature we long for closeness.

Yet we are prone to pose.

Pretend.

Hide.

Keep everybody at arms length.

Settle for shallow.

Yet our souls need deep, transparent, laughter-filled, tear-filled friendship.

And it won't just happen.

We gotta go get it.

Here's how to go get it:

Of course pray. Ask God to bring you some close friends. Ask. Ask a person or a small group of people to join you on this journey of companionship. I know this sounds a bit goofy and maybe even creepy, but if you don't ask you'll never know.

Commit. Life is busy. If you don't fight for times to gather it will not happen.

Risk. Risk being vulnerable with somebody or somebodies. Don't keep it surfacey. Open the closet and let them see the skeletons.

It's worth it.

Go get it!

Friends 3
By Rob Link

I remember a few years ago when my depression was getting the best of me. Two of my closest friends responded to a call from my wife, Kristy, and came and dragged me out of my basement and my stupor and made me walk the disc golf course with disc in hand. It was just what I needed.

I'm thinking of the two couples Kristy and I hang out with regularly, the Lukes and the Resh's. Without question our marriage is richer, stronger, deeper, freer, and more solid because of them.

I'm recalling my days back in seminary and how I felt like a fish out of water – until I meet my pal Mike. I'm not sure how I could have made it through those three years with out his companionship.

Laughing.

Crying.

Yelling.

Growing.

Life is better with friends.

What do you need to do to make such friendships happen?

Winning Battles
by Rod Tucker

"The Lord will fight for you; you need only to be still."
Exodus 14:14

Some of the greatest battles in the Bible are won, not because the warriors were strong and mighty, but because the warriors trusted the Lord.

David beat Goliath because he trusted God.

Gideon defeated the opposing army because he trusted God.

There are many stories in the Bible where people trusted God and, as a result, won the battle.

"Not by might nor by power, but by my Spirit," says the LORD Almighty.
Zechariah 4:6b

No matter what battle you are in, you are not going to win it on your own. God will help you if you can only seek him, be still, and trust that he will do what is best because he loves you.

What "battles" are you facing right now?

What help do you need?

Pray and ask God to fight for you.

Tryouts
by Rob Link

My friend Rod and I have co-coached the 8th grade basketball team at Maple Street Middle School for a few years. The worst part about coaching – tryouts.

It is a yucky thing to tell several young men who have had high hopes and who have worked hard that their level of skill simply isn't where it needs to be to make the 8th grade team.

Over the years I've seen many a young man cry and many others pretend not too.

This, in a word, stinks.

From the beginning of tryouts we try to soften the impending blow by heaping on the kindness, by assuring them their worth as a human has nothing to do with the ability to play a game, and by exuding as much warmth as possible.

But it still stinks.

It certainly stinks for Rod and me. Nobody likes to be the cause of someone else's pain.

It stinks for the parents of the young men who do not make the team. No parent wants to see his or her son (or daughter) hurt.

Most of all it stinks for the young man. No matter how hard we try to affirm, it is still a rejection.

It stinks.

Unfortunately life is filled with such rejections.

Many of you have felt it over the years.

Maybe it was back in the elementary school where you didn't fit in. Those scars still hurt.

Maybe it was middle school where your awkward self couldn't jive with your peers. For many those taunts still echo in the old noggin.

Maybe it was in high school where you had the misfortune of not being able to afford the "right" style of jeans and/or shoes. Damage done. Still haunts.

Or maybe you are still in school and the stinking described in the prior 2 paragraphs is your current reality. Ouch.

Maybe it was a your parents divorce, abuse, a failed marriage…

Rejection.

Stinks.

What if there was a place where there was no rejection.

What if there was a place where your style, skills, awkwardness, etc. made no difference on your acceptance.

What if there was a place where anyone would be accepted just because acceptance was the norm.

What if I told you there is such a place.

There is.

In the presence of Jesus.

Look how he treated folks in the Bible. Anytime he came into contact with the rejected he provided acceptance.

Anytime he came in contact with the rejecters he provided rebuke and correction.

Here's the deal. Jesus is and his followers (i.e. the church) ought to be the safest place on earth.

So if you are feeling the rejection of life, walk into His presence.

If you are a follower of Jesus and find yourself rejecting folks, stop it.

When and where have you felt rejection?

When and where have you offered rejection to another?

What do you think it means to "walk into His presence?"

No Second Class Citizens
by Jason Luke

South Africa was a country where the whites had been lording over the blacks for hundreds of years. A transition period came, led by political activist Nelson Mandela. Mandela, like Dr. Martin Luther King Jr., wanted change. In attempts to challenge or rise against this social injustice, Mandela was imprisoned for 27 years.

Did you catch that – 27 years?

We struggle missing lunch, or throw a fit when we don't get to watch our show, or go into a rage when someone cuts us off while driving.

Mandela spent a fourth of his life in a prison cell about the size of your closet.

So what happened to him during that time? How angry would you be? Here he is standing up for what is right only to be jailed. Mandela took a supernatural approach to his imprisonment. It's only by God's power and a deep understanding of grace that he came out of prison not seeking revenge, but wanting to better his country.

After being released, he got elected to be the first black President of South Africa. One of his biggest challenges was to reboot the minds of a people group who had considered themselves to be less than others. Examine the words that he delivers in his 1994 inaugural presidential address:

> Our deepest fear is not that we are inadequate. Our deepest fear is that we are powerful beyond measure. It is our Light, not our Darkness, that most frightens us. We ask ourselves, who am I to be brilliant, gorgeous, talented, fabulous? Actually, who are you NOT to be? You are a child of God. Your playing small does not serve the world. There is nothing enlightened about shrinking so that other people won't feel insecure around you. We are born to make manifest the glory of God that is within us. It is not just in some of us; it is in everyone. And as we let our own Light shine, we unconsciously give other people permission to do the same. As we are liberated from our own fear, our presence automatically liberates others.

Wow, did you hear that? Talk about empowering. He had the nerve to ask them to begin to recognize their God given value. He knew that unless there was a shift in their self-worth, no government regulations could prevent this second-class mentality.

You are no second-class citizen either!

"You are a child of God. Your playing small does not serve the world."

Do you know what it means to be a son of the King of Kings? If so, how do you show this?

What words in Mandela's speech are most empowering to you? Why?

Beard
by Rob Link

Have you ever seen a photograph of an Eastern Orthodox priest?

Go Google it right now.

You'll notice he has a sweet beard.

And an awesome robe.

What you can't see is that in addition to a sweet beard and awesome robe, he can speak multiple languages.

To be an Eastern Orthodox priest, you need to know Hebrew, Greek, Aramaic, and Latin.

Impressive.

You have to study for years and years to be ordained as an Eastern Orthodox priest.

What about a Jewish priest? Go ahead and Google-image that too.

He also sports a nice robe.

And an impressive beard.

Jewish boys could not even be considered for priestly training until they were twelve years old. By age twelve they would have to have memorized the first five books of the Bible word-for-word. If at age twelve they did not show the mental acuity to do such a thing, no priest's robe for them.

But the beard was still a possibility.

And then there are Catholic priests.

These guys, in addition to having nice robes (few beards), have to study years and years before they can become ordained. They also need to be fluent in – not just familiar with, but fluent in – Latin. In addition to studying for years and being able to speak Latin, they must take several vows. They take a vow of poverty, a vow to own nothing and simply live by the good graces of the people they serve.

And they take a vow of celibacy.

Bummer.

But you have to do such things if you want to be a Catholic priest.

Regardless of what your religion is, to be a priest you have to give years and years and years of study.

It's true for us Protestant types too.

In order for me to be an ordained pastor in the Reformed Church in America I had to have a four-year degree. I went to Ferris State University and got a counseling degree. Then I had to go to seminary for three years after getting my college degree to get a master's degree. Studying for that master's degree, I learned the ancient Hebrew language. I also had to learn ancient Greek. (FYI, I subsequently forgot the Hebrew and Greek languages.) I had to study the art of communication known as preaching. In addition to getting at least a B average for three straight years, the seminary had to sign off after I took a psychological examination. I had to pay eight hundred dollars for them to evaluate whether I was mentally stable enough to be a pastor.

Don't say anything; I passed. Thank you.

And on my first assignment fresh out of seminary, on the first day, they told me to stand still and stretch my arms out. They measured me from head to toe for my custom-fit robe.

Yes, my very own robe.

The beard came later.

All of that information on priests is to say this: you don't have the training.

I want to remind you that in most of the world's religions to be a priest is a special and elite thing.

In case you are not clear, leave the work of God to the professionals.

Leave the work of the kingdom of God to those who have paid their dues with long years of education and who own robes.

Don't you think for a minute that you could serve as a priest in the kingdom of God!

Right?

Wrong!

In the book of 1 Peter, chapter 2, verse 5, it says, "You also, like living stones, are being built into a spiritual house to be a holy priesthood." You are being built into a spiritual house to be a holy priesthood.

What?! Who is he talking to?

Peter is talking to untrained, un-bearded (well, they might have had beards), un-expert people – not a robe in sight – and he is saying that because of the work of the Holy Spirit, they are being trained to be priests.

What about the years of training, the years of study, the sacrifices?

What about the need for an awesome robe?!

You don't need any of that to be priest, a laborer in God's kingdom (although a beard might help).

God has given you an assignment that only you can fulfill. There are folks in your world who need the life and joy that is only found in Jesus. So get to it.

Don't wait for the professionals to do it. You do it.

And if it would help, I have a custom made robe that has

been hanging untouched for years in the closet I could let you borrow.

Can you grow a beard? It doesn't matter.

Where has God called you to be a "priest?"

Risk

by Brian Fraaza

I grew up being afraid to risk. Somewhere in my elementary years, I became deathly afraid of what other people thought of me and this caused me to live being petrified of doing anything that carried the risk of being humiliated. I missed out on a lot of really cool, fun things because of this. I never excelled in athletics because I was afraid to fail. I never had a lot of friends because I was afraid to really be myself and lay it all on the line for fear of rejection. My insecurities became a sort of master, controlling virtually every aspect of how I lived my life.

The first glimpse of something different came when I began to play music. At first I would make sure that no one ever heard me play so that I wouldn't be judged. Eventually, a few people heard me play 'accidently' and they loved it. That began to grow confidence in me to play in front of more people. Over time, I began to realize that playing music brought a ton of joy to me and it gave a ton of joy to others. What would have happened if those first few people had never heard me? If I would never had taken the risky step of letting others hear me play, it's entirely possible that I would have stopped altogether because the joy and purpose in the music would have been shallow and short-lived.

So, yes. I am telling you to risk cool-ness, pain and humiliation. Sometimes, even risk personal injury… Because in the end, if you're not willing to risk for the reward of things that don't really matter much, you won't know how to risk on the things that do.

What are some areas that you have an opportunity to take a risk?

What opportunities have you let pass you by because you were afraid to risk?

Barkly
by Rob Link

We love celebrating Barkly's birthday.

We always have big plans. It's not everyday that our beloved newfy has a birthday.

We take him to McDonalds for 3 hamburgers (he's big, 175 lbs. 3 burgers are just a light snack for him). Then we go to the pet store and buy him a bone and a few pig ears (he thinks they are tasty). Then we take him to the dog park for a romp with his buddies.

It's always a big day.

The kids and I get pumped to celebrate our dogs birthday.

I know. I know. It's kinda crazy. Sorta nuts.

Or is it.

Let's think biblically for a minute and see if our dog party has a theological leg to stand on.

(I want to say real quick that some of you non "animal people" won't get this. But those of you who consider yourselves "animal people" – whether you are a dog, cat, or horse person – might resonate with the following.)

Point 1: Way back when Adam and Eve were chillin' in the garden, they lived in close proximity to animals. In Eden, there was no tension or animosity between the first couple and the critters. In fact you could say that they lived in perfect harmony.

Point 2: After the flood, when Noah and his family left the ark, God made a covenant with *all of creation* – not just the people. His covenant was to not wipe out creation again. The Bible is clear that the covenant included more than just people. All of creation included animals. Check it out for yourself.

Point 3: At the end of time (see Revelation 21) God will create a new heaven and new earth. Eden will be restored. Check that out too. It's in the Bible. Eden will be restored. Restored. To the way it was. People living in perfect harmony with creation – including the critters.

With these 3 biblical thoughts in mind, here is some doggie theology: when we have a close connection with an animal be it a dog (like the Links celebrating Barkly), a cat, a horse, etc. we are really living out of the echo of how we were intended to live – in perfect harmony with creation.

Let me say it this way: the human/animal bond that many of us feel (not all do, that's ok) is a reflection of what was (Eden) and what will be (Heaven).

Barkly gives me and my kids a taste of Eden and a glimpse of Heaven.

I think this is good, biblical theology.

So if your kids have been asking for that pet and you've been hesitant, maybe it is time to give em a taste of Eden and a glimpse of Heaven.

Of course, not all will resonate.

That's OK.

After all it's hard to see Eden through the slobber, stinky fur, and poop in the yard.

What was your first pet?

How has your pet(s) both current and past given you a glimpse of Eden?

The Last Crusade
by Rob Link

I recently saw a cool, old clip from *Indiana Jones: The Last Crusade*. Indiana is on the last leg in his hunt for the Holy Grail. The scene I watched showed him standing on the edge of a bottomless canyon 30 yards across with no way across. The bummer for good ole Indiana is that he needs to get to the other side to retrieve the grail (and save his dad's life).

With the words from his dads notebook encouraging him to have faith, he steps blindly off the ledge…only to discover there is a stone bridge that is made of the same stone as the opposite wall forming an optical illusion. Where it looked like there was no way, there actually was a way. Where it looked like there was no way, there actually was a way.

Hmmm…

Reminds me of a story from the Biblical book of 2 Kings. There is a huge army set against God's people. The Prophet of God is relaxed. His servant is freaking out.

The servant is freaking out because he sees no way out of this problem.

Elisha (the prophet) prayed that God would open the servant's eyes.

They were.

And he saw something.

Where it looked like there was no way, there actually was a way.

The servant saw that the Angel Army of God far out numbered the enemy.

The servant stopped freaking out.

With both Indiana Jones and this Old Testament story in mind, I'm wondering if there is something that we aren't seeing.

Is there something we are missing?

In the midst of the difficulty of life, could it be that there is still a God in heaven who has an Army fighting on our behalf?

Could it be that when it seems there is no way, there is actually a rock solid path right in front of us?

Could it be that one single step of faith could open up a whole new world before us?

Could it be?

I think so.

Where it looks like there is no way, there actually is a way.

Who knew Indiana Jones was such a good theologian.

Do you resonate with Elisha's servant? Does "freaking out" describe you?

What is causing you to freak out these days (if anything)?

Pray and ask God to open your eyes.

Courage
by Rob Link

I was hanging out with a couple pastor friends of mine a while ago.

These were not your normal run of the mill type of pastors. They were both cutting edge in what they were doing. Both had started new congregations that were populated with broken people who would otherwise not be comfortable in the usual church. These were men that people were naturally drawn too (unfortunately a rare trait among pastors).

And they were happy.

So was I.

There we were. Three happy, content, joy filled pastors. One of us (I don't remember who) noted the fact that we were happy, content, and joy filled.

Another noted how rare that was for a group of pastors.

We began to sadly list a boatload of pastor friends of ours

who were not happy.

The list was long.

What was the difference we wondered?? Why were we happy when so many were not? We were each of a different race/ethnicity. So that wasn't the key. We each worked in different locations. So that wasn't the common factor. What was it that led us to be content when so many pastors are not?

One of my friends made an astute observation. He observed that each one of us had at one time been working in a comfortable, suburban type church where every one was clean and tidy. We had stable paychecks and steady normal services.

And each one of us left and moved to the run down part of our respective cities. We each said no to the stable and steady and started something new. As a result each of us had a sweet church where the homeless sat next to the home owner, where the unemployed sat next to the employed, where poor mingled with wealth, where black mixed with white. We each serve in an exciting church where lives are changed regularly and people find freedom on a daily basis.

Yet this fact wasn't the key to our joy. There was something before all of this.

That something was courage.

Courage.

To be honest, none of us said to ourselves, "I need to do the courageous thing." By God's grace and our different circumstances we stumbled into the courageous act of leaving the safe and comfortable and embarking upon the risky and unknown. As a result we each found ourselves in a good place.

All because of courage.

Here's the deal; what is true for three pastors is true for you.

The comfortable, easy way is not the way to a joy filled life.

Risking is better than comfy living.

We were made for adventure, not apathy.

I wonder what risk you are being called too? I wonder

where you have chosen easy and comfortable over risk and courage?

It's a new day. Make a courageous decision and watch your joy level rise.

Which describes you best: comfortable, easy or courageous, adventurous?

What risk are you facing?

Grumpy
by Rob Link

I had one of those weeks.

You know what I'm talking about, I'm sure.

Kristy and I were not connecting, bickering over stupid stuff – on my insistence not hers.

I was grumpy with the kids through no fault of their own – just me being a knucklehead.

I didn't want to go to our bi weekly gathering with friends – not because the friends were no longer awesome, I was just feeling crabby.

It was during basketball season. As mentioned earlier, I coach 8th grade basketball and usually love it. Couldn't stand it on this particular week. Not because of the young men. I was just in a grumpy mood.

I usually love running a few miles several times a week. That week running seemed like a stupid idea.

You know what I'm talking about don't you.

You've had such weeks. I know you have.

Some of you are in the midst of such a week right now aren't you?

Fortunately my days eventually took a turn for the better.

One week I was feeling grumpy and bickery.

The very next week I wasn't.

On the contrary I felt light hearted, joyful.

What's the cause of the difference?

Intimacy with Jesus.

As sure as any snake oil huckster of old would proclaim at the top of his lungs his cure-all tonic, I want you to hear about the cure I've found (for the hundredth time) for my grumpy, curmudgeonly days – peace filled quiet time sitting and talking to God.

Intimacy.

With God.

I don't know if a daily dose of prayer will cure all that ails you, but I do know it brings peace where peace is lacking, joy where joy is missing, and perspective where perspective is absent.

If you are having one of those weeks, give it a try.

Describe your last grumpy week (it might be right now).

Take some time to sit with Jesus.

God vs. Stuff
by Rod Tucker

Keep your lives free from the love of money and be content with what you have, because God has said, "Never will I leave you; never will I forsake you." Hebrews 13:5

God will always take care of us. He tells us that he will in his word.

"Look at the birds of the air; they do not sow or reap or store away in barns, and yet your heavenly Father feeds them. Are you not much more valuable than they?" Matthew 6:26

The love of money will not allow us to be content with what we have. If we love money we will always want more and what we have will never be enough.

God desires us to be content because he loves us, not because we have a bunch of stuff. God is so much greater than stuff and he wants us to know how much he loves us. Sometimes it can be difficult for us to see and understand how much God cares for us when our lives are filled with things.

When we begin to love money and things, we forget about God. However, God never forgets about us and will always remind us to get rid of stuff so that we can better see him and know how much he loves us.

What "things" compete with God in your life?

Having read this devotional what do you feel you should do about those things?

Void Within
by Rob Link

Some old dead guy once said, "we all have a God-shaped void inside of us."

Hmmm…

What do you think? Could it be true?

Is there really a deep longing for something deeper, something bigger in all of us that only God can fulfill?

What do you think?

Could it be that those moments of awe, wonder, amazement are those moments when that void is unknowingly filled with the presence of the almighty?

That moment when your first child is born.

Your wedding day.

Laughing with close friends.

Sitting by the Christmas tree quietly late at night.

Watching the sun slip peacefully below the horizon.

Walking with your dog as the snow falls in big, fat flakes.

Could it be that these moments of transcendent peace are the moments we are closest to the creator of the world?

Today we have more things to fill our time than any other time in human history.

iPads, iPods, iPhones.

Cable, Satellite, Hulu, Netflix.

Yet as a people, we are more bored and purposeless than ever.

It might just be because these things don't touch on that "god-shaped void." It might be that they keep us from the pursuit of filling the void with awe and wonder.

It seems like it would be a good idea to turn off the stuff that entertains and tune in to the stuff that marvels.

When was the last time you experienced a moment of awe, wonder, and amazement?

What things cause you to stop and ponder God's goodness?

What things get in the way of this?

Principal
by Dori Beltz

I remember a few years ago when my third grade daughter was trying to earn the privilege of being "principal for a day".

Having a third grader run the school just seemed like a bad idea.

Declaring all day recess and demanding cookies for lunch – actually, that wouldn't have been so terrible.

What about a cupcake baker being "auto mechanic for a day"?

Or a sumo wrestler being "ballerina for a day"?

I'm pretty sure people should just stick to doing what they've been gifted and trained to do. We all have a purpose, even though sometimes it's a challenge to figure out what it is!

What are you good at?

What do you enjoy?

How has God wired you?

What gives you purpose?

God is our creator and He is the creator of our purpose. He makes cupcake bakers and auto mechanics, sumo wrestlers and ballerinas.

He made you and me.

Romans 8:28 says it like this:

> *"And we know that in all things God works for the good of those who love him, who have been called according to his purpose."*

So God works too. He works for our good.

He works. We work.

And we definitely shouldn't get our jobs mixed up! No one has had success being "God for a day". Many have tried (including myself) and really made a mess of things.

Whatever you do, do it well. Do it to his glory.

And leave the running of the universe to God.

Grudge
by Rob Link

I've realized something about myself; I'm really good at something that really isn't good. Even though I am good at this thing I really want to get bad at it.

I'm good at holding a grudge.

That's not good.

In fact it's bad.

Here's the deal; if someone offends, hurts, annoys, bothers, or in anyway harms me – I will hold a grudge.

That grudge looks like this; when I see the offending person I will…

Avoid them.

Pretend like I didn't see them in the grocery store when I know they have seen me.

Think poorly of them.

Talk poorly of them (thinly guised as a prayer concern).

Write them off.

Yes, I am good at holding a grudge.

I even have a physical reaction in my gut when I see the grudgee.

This is bad.

Not only is it bad, it's stupid.

Someone once said that holding a grudge is like drinking rat poison and expecting someone else to get sick.

It's true. Being bitter and holding onto past wrongs (real or perceived) does bad things to the one holding on.

It robs us.

Yes I said *us*, because I'm not the only one good at this. Many of you are professional grade grudge holders too. You know who you are.

It robs us of joy, peace, health – both physical and emotional, causes angst, raises blood pressure, ends relationships…I could go on.

Thus it is stupid.

It's also stupid because no one is perfect. Sooner or later everyone we are in relationship with will hurt us (most likely unintentionally). If we hold a grudge against everyone who offends us we will eventually have no one we are not holding a grudge against!

For crying out loud! This is stupid.

And yet I am really good at it.

So a while back I decided to do something to help me become bad at this not-good thing that I am currently good at.

I made a list.

A list of all the people I have been holding a grudge against.

And slowly I've been working down that list, meeting with the individuals and – are you ready for this craziness?! – Apologizing for holding a grudge.

Crazy.

Something has happened every single time. Several something's actually.

Each and every time.

The person is usually shocked.

They have always offered forgiveness for my grudge holding.

They have asked what they did to prompt the grudge.

I've answered that question.

They have expressed remorse.

They have asked for forgiveness.

I have forgiven.

The relationship has been restored.

Crazy. Every time. No exception.

People want restoration and wholeness.

Why don't you make your own list.

Then slowly but surely work your way out of grudge-holding.

People of Grace
by Rob Link

Christmas. What a great time of year.

It's an even better theological proposition.

Get this: Christianity espouses that we are all sinful and thus separated from God. Yet God longs to be in relationship with us, but our sinfulness keeps us from that tight communion with God we were created for. Seems like an insurmountable conundrum.

Until you throw Christmas in the mix.

God's solution to the human sin problem was to take on flesh, walk this earth as a man – a sinless man, take the punishment of sin in our place via the cross and death, and burst out of the tomb conquering death and the effect of sin.

Amazing when you think about it.

Simply amazing.

God's grace and mercy (and our surrender, repentance, and embracing His grace and mercy) equals life and freedom for us.

Free of charge.

Not earned.

Given.

Grace.

Awesome.

Merry Christmas! (No matter what month it is.)

Therefore since we know we are sinners, saved by grace we can be kind, open, courteous, loving, generous, compassionate, humble, gentle, patient, and nice people.

Even with those who believe differently than us.

Even with those who vote differently than us.

Even with those whose lifestyle is different than ours.

With all people.

Kind, open, courteous, loving, generous, compassionate, humble, gentle, patient, and nice.

With all people.

All people.

The fact of the matter is that God didn't take on a people-suit, wear diapers, die on a cross, go kick death's butt so we could be rude and mean to people who are different than us!

Because of the grace exhibited at Christmas we do not need to patrol the world's belief systems as if we have been appointed the doctrine police.

We do not need to force, manipulate, or coerce anyone into believing Jesus is who he said he was.

There is no need for us to scream at the world what our moral standard is and thus what the worlds ought to be.

No, as sinners saved by grace we need only be people who walk in and live out grace.

Because of grace, because of Christmas we can be kind, open, courteous, loving, generous, compassionate, humble, gentle, patient, and nice.

To all people.

How/where has grace transformed you?

Resolution
by Rob Link

Have you ever made a New Years Resolution?

Let me fill you in on what these resolutions really are.

They are guilt pits that lurk in disguise for a while only to jump on us later during the year. They cruelly remind us of our failures and short-comings. They remind us of our inability to break through. They tell us that when left to our own devices we will fail.

Yuck.

I'll pass, thank you very much.

Yet it is a good idea to refine ourselves. We'd like to walk in a bit more freedom. It would be really sweet if we could experience victory in areas where victory has been lacking.

You'd like to be refined, wouldn't you?

Of course you would.

Just without all the guilt and shame.

The Bible tells us that we can do all things through Christ who strengthens us.

It also says that if we seek God, His Kingdom, and His righteousness that He will add all things to us. But only after we seek Him.

Hmmmm…

Why don't we do this then: instead of making a list of 78 resolutions that will only lead to guilt, let's make one that will lead to life.

Let's simply resolve to seek God.

He won't be hard to find. He tells us in His Word that if we seek we will find.

So are you in?

If so, how you going to do it?

A Bible reading plan?

Start a prayer journal?

Bible on CD for that morning commute?

Pop in a worship CD for the drive home?

Make church a priority?

Whatever and however know that you can do all things through Christ and that if you seek Him first He will add all things to your life.

Have You Ever Heard of the Person?
by Dan Smith

We live in a time period where information is readily available at the blink of an eye. Conversations and connectivity with each other is at our fingertips. As a Christ-follower I have increasingly seen many of us make excuses for why people do not respond to the Gospel. Oftentimes we blame ourselves or other Christians that have painted a bad picture of who Christ is, and who he is for people everywhere. This is true. However, what I know to be even truer is that I believe Christians across the world, even pastors and church leaders have turned to philosophies that do not depend on the Word of God. We lean on our great music, our cool environment, our coffee shops, and our unique buildings to show seekers how much God loves them.

There are great tools, but none of those things will prosper a marriage. None of those things will rescue someone from any kind of abuse. None of those things will lead someone to serve selflessly. If anything, it makes people want more me, me, me. We are the church, we are different, we should offer hope and more importantly we should be teaching people to obey everything he has commanded us.

"Therefore go and make disciples of all nations, baptizing them in the name of the Father and of the Son and of the Holy Spirit, and teaching them to obey everything I have commanded you. And surely I am with you always, to the very end of the age."
Matthew 28:19-20

The world can offer great music, great coffee, and awesome environments to be a part of, but the Kingdom offers eternal freedom that begins now for anyone who would follow.

Are we leading people to follow? Or are we scared that non-Christ followers have all of these bad feelings towards us as Christians?

Have you ever heard of any person who has screwed up their life by following God's will?

In Secure
by Rob Link

There's a myth out there that I want to debunk. And in so doing I'm going to blow the cover of man kind (yes I mean man kind, as in male, gender specific). Sorry fellas.

The myth: insecurity is a woman-only struggle. Go ahead and do a Google image (safe search on please) search of the word "insecure." A vast majority of the images are feminine in nature. (Full disclosure: there was one image of Darth Vader under the search "insecure." Other than that the images were womanly.) The myth is that insecurity is a thing for the ladies only.

The Truth: it's not.

Let me say it again. It. Is. Not.

Men struggle with insecurities in great measure. Oh we might try to bluster our way through life hoping no one discovers our hidden fears. But the fact of the matter is dudes have as many, if not more, insecurities as women.

Here's a partial list of my insecurities to help prove my

point. Mind you this is only a partial list:

1. My waistline is larger than it used to be – yuck. A few extra pounds a year has made my pants tighter than I'd like. I hate that. I know from looking at the dudes on the magazine covers as well as seeing the hugely muscled action figures my kids have played with that my physique is less than right.

2. My beard has more white in it now that black. My goodness if this and insecurity number 1 keeps up I'll look like Santa in a few short years. Trust me – no guy wants to look like Santa.

3. I don't smile cause my teeth aren't white enough.

4. I get nervous in a crowd for fear of not being likable enough.

5. Although I shave my head I only do so because it is (in my opinion) a better option than the comb over or old man horseshoe-do. I wish I had a full, thick head of hair and inwardly hate every man above forty who does. Well maybe not hate, but certainly I'm angrily jealous.

6. And then there is the family. My word. A whole other

set of insecurities arise there.

    a. Am I a good enough husband?

    b. Am I raising my kids right?

    c. Can I provide financially for them?

    d. Can I provide emotionally for my wife and kids?

    e. Am I doing the right things to raise healthy kids?

    f. Why can't I speak my wife's love language well?

7. I'm even insecure about admitting I am insecure for crying out loud!

Men admit it. Women trust me. Insecurity is a thing for the fellas too.

Famed 21st century poet, Eminem, has said, "my insecurities could eat me alive."

Yep. Mine too.

Here is what I am wondering. Am I, are we, destined to a life of icky thoughts when it comes to evaluating ourselves?

Are we?

I don't think so. God thinks much more highly of us that we do. Read this Bible stuff:

"Therefore, as God's chosen people, holy and dearly loved…" – What?! We are **dearly loved**?!

"You knit me together in my mother's womb. I praise you because I am fearfully and wonderfully made" – Really?! We were wonderfully made by God?!

"See what great love the Father has lavished on us, that we should be called **children** of **God**!" God boldly calls us his kids?! Even with male pattern baldness and expanding waistlines?!

Think about this. The whole Christian faith is built around the theology of a God who loved his messed up people so much that he went to unheard of extremes just to be reunited with them! He likes us that much! Our insecurities are non-issues to him.

Amazing.

If all of that is true (which I think it is) how in the world do we rid ourselves of those horrible inner voices that scream loudly at us?

The answer my friends is blowin' in the winds, err, well not really. (Sorry for the Bob Dylan reference, but aren't you a little impressed? Both Bob Dylan and Eminem referenced in one devotional. Thank you very much.)

The answer is not blowin' in the wind. Rather it can be found in the words of Jesus.

"But **seek first** the **kingdom** of **God** and his righteousness, and all these things will be added to you."

I know this to be true. When I take some time each day (doesn't even have to be a ton of time) to read a bit of the Bible, pray, and listen for that still small voice the insecurities are much less loud.

Give it a try. See if you find yourself a bit less insecure and a bit more in Christ secure.

What insecurities do you have?

Have you ever shared them with someone?

Do so today.

Table Manner Challenge
by Rob Link

Question: In what manner do you use your table?

Do you use it as a desk to pay bills?

Do the kids sit at it grudgingly plodding through homework?

Is it a junk collector, catching any piece of stray mail or clutter that comes within 10 feet?

In what manner do you use your table?

Did you know you could actually eat dinner with your family and/or friends at the table?

It's true. You can. I've done it before.

And so have you.

In fact I'll bet many of you have some fond memories from the table.

How many of you sat down for family dinner when you were younger? Do you remember sharing stories of the day while being forced to eat your veggies? In spite of the veggies you probably have at least a few good memories.

Do you remember grandma's house at Thanksgiving? Even if you were banished to the kid table I'll bet you have some good memories.

The fact of the matter is eating and bonding go hand in hand.

Did you know that according to The Family Dinner Challenge Research Department, 89.9% of American families believe it is "very important" to eat together as a family?

Yet according to a Gallup poll only 47% of families eat together 4-6 times a week.

Bottom line – we all know it's a good thing. It's just hard to do. We could take hours listing all the things that compete with table time. No need. We all know.

Another fact for you – some things are worth fighting for.

Here's some motivational fuel to add to the fight.

According to The National Center on Addiction and Substance Abuse at Columbia University, kids and teens who share family dinners three or more times per week:

- Are more likely to eat healthy food
- Are less likely to be overweight
- Perform better academically
- Are less likely to engage in risky behaviors (drugs, alcohol, sexual activity)
- Have better relationships with their parents

Another study shows evidence that family dinners increase mental health and decrease depression and anxiety.

Table manners matter!

Here's some Bible motivation for you:

- The word table is used 75 times in the scriptures – almost always as a place to gather.
- The very last thing Jesus did before he went to the cross was to gather his friends at a table (note for you who are not married and don't have kids – neither did Jesus, yet the table still mattered to him!)
- The very first time Jesus appeared to his disciples as a group they were gathered around a table.

Table manners matter.

I wonder if you would be up for a challenge, a task, a little adventure?

Would you be up for trying for 7 weeks to eat together as a family at least 4 times each week? Or if you are not married, eat at least 4 meals a week with someone at a table?

Let's call it **The Table Manner Challenge**.

If you are nervous on what to do during the table time, simply ask each person to share the Hi's of the day and the Lo's. Hi/lo. That's it.

Will you take the challenge?

Salt of the Earth
by Jud Collins

I'm going to be very honest with you – my adolescent years stunk.

I did well in school, played some sports, and had a few friends, but I didn't really know who I was.

There is so much pressure to figure out who you're supposed to be, but how are you really supposed to know?

Most of the cool kids were mean. Most of the artistic kids were into all kinds of things I didn't want to be part of. And many of the other kids weren't very much fun. There just seemed to be something off, no matter what group of people I tried to hang out with. I felt like I had to pick what group I wanted to be in, and then force myself to fit the mold for that group. It was hard, and no fun.

What I didn't know – what I wish someone would have told me – is that I had it all backwards.

It is not our job to shape ourselves to fit into the world

around us; it is our job to shape the world around us to fit ourselves.

That's the power of the Holy Spirit inside you.

There's a verse in the Bible where Jesus says, "You are the salt of the earth" (Matthew 5:13).

I don't even like salt, so I never really got what that meant.

Now I finally know that it's not really about the taste of salt – it's about the way salt preserves meat. Did you know that, before refrigeration was invented, people would cover meat with salt to keep it from rotting? A few sprinkles of salt here and there will keep a piece of meat from going bad, even if it's not in the fridge. So when Jesus calls you the salt of the earth, he means that your spirit keeps the rest of the world from becoming too rotten.

A few guys with the Spirit of God in them scattered throughout a group will make the entire group better.

And you know the best part?

You don't even have to do anything!

Just be close to Jesus.

If you know him and follow him, that's enough. Stand up when you don't feel like something is right, but don't feel like you have to go out of your way to make everyone do the right thing. If you just lead by example like Jesus does, God takes care of the rest.

So if you don't feel like you fit in, good.

You don't.

But that's awesome. Instead of trying to fit in, read your Bible, especially the parts where Jesus is speaking. Then live in a way that goes along with what you read.

I read my Bible every day, even the same parts over and over. The more I learn about Jesus, the more I like him. And the closer I feel to him. I don't have to force myself to fit a mold for him, and that's totally awesome. And now when the world feels rotten around me, I can step up, be the salt, and watch God clean things up. It's a lot easier this way!

Where do you see rotten things around you? How can you be the salt that keeps the meat fresh?

Where are you trying to fit in that isn't very much fun for you? What would happen if you stopped?

Insides
by Rob Link

I was at a gas station a while back getting an ice-cold Mt. Dew.

When I set the sweet nectar of heaven on the counter to pay, I engaged the dude working in a brief bit of conversation. He said something that caught me off guard.

"Are you an under cover cop?" he asked.

"No. Why?" I responded.

"You sound way more intelligent than you look. Way more!"

Read that again.

He said I sounded way more intelligent than I looked! What?! Who says such things?

I just about dropped my Mt. Dew. (Which would have been a crime.)

It was clear that he had made some snap judgments about me solely based on appearance. In his mind, those judgments were 100% accurate.

Until I spoke.

His preconceived notions were shattered.

And he was shocked.

So shocked, in fact, that he blurted out his inane and potentially hurtful comment utterly aghast. He was surprised – to say the least – and mildly scandalized that his adjudication could be wrong.

Driving away chuckling to myself at his absurdity I began to think the following thought;

Most of us are like the gas station attendant.

Me.

You.

Whereas we might not speak our crazy thoughts like he did, we often lump people into a category simply based on outward appearance. We see a person and make a snap decision on who they are and whether or not they are worth our time. By simply noting clothing, style, hair, hygiene, etc. we draw conclusions that in our mind are 100% precise.

And that's stupid.

Plain old stupid.

How in the world can we know what is on the inside of a man by mere appearance? How can we judge the character of a woman simply by noting her fashion or lack thereof?

How?

We can't. That's how.

There's this passage in the Old Testament book of 1 Samuel that says, "people look at the outward appearance, but God looks at the heart."

Driving away from the gas station that night I had two thoughts;

1. I was a lot like the attendant, but I would rather be like God.

2. Mt. Dew is tasty.

When have you felt judged solely on your appearance?

When have you judged someone solely on their appearance?

Courage
by Rod Tucker

> *"Have I not commanded you? Be strong and courageous. Do not be afraid; do not be discouraged, for the Lord your God will be with you wherever you go."*
> *Joshua 1:9*

God wants us to be courageous in everything we do, and he has given us the power to be so. The key to being successful for God's Kingdom is in seeking him to find out what he wants you to do, and then praying for boldness as you step into his leading.

This is why The Apostle Paul asked people to pray for him for fearlessness.

> *"Pray also for me, that whenever I speak, words may be given me so that I will fearlessly make known the mystery of the gospel…"*
> *Ephesians 6:19*

"All you need is twenty seconds of insane courage, and I promise you, something great will come of it." – *We Bought a Zoo* (2012)

"There is more in us than we know. If we can be made to see it perhaps for the rest of our lives we will be unwilling to settle for less." – Kurt Hahn

How high or low is your courage level?

When was the last time you needed courage?

When scared, what is your normal response?

Incognito Chicken
by Rob Link

I'm a chicken.

Yet I fool myself into thinking I'm noble.

Crazy.

I'm a chicken in my marriage, at work, while parenting, in my friendships.

One big, pretending-to-be-noble chicken.

I don't have my wallet on me, but if I did I would bet $3 you are too.

You big chicken.

Pretending to be noble.

Here's why. I pretend to overlook something that has hurt, bothered, annoyed, or bugged me saying to myself, "well it isn't that big of a deal and _____ (fill in the blank:

spouse, co worker, child, friend, etc.) probably didn't mean to do it."

Then I say to myself, "wow, you are very impressive, a venerable gift to humanity, overlooking that thing like that. The world really needs more people like you."

To be sure overlooking an offense is a noble thing to do at times. But not always. It is noble only if I (we) can overlook the offense and simply let it go.

The key phrase is, "let it go."

That's hard to do. The norm for me is to not let it go and silently hold onto that thing that that person did. As the days and years go by, those little things add up and I keep saying to myself, "no big deal." Eventually I have enough of "no big deals" accumulated that I either:

    A. Explode in anger
    B. Avoid the person
    C. Harbor a grudge
    D. Think less of the offender

All because I pretended to be noble and never said anything. This "noble" silence is deadly to relationships and is avoidable.

When I'm deep down honest I see that my silence really isn't my gifting humanity with my awesomeness. Rather it is me being a big ole chicken.

Bok bok.

All those awkward relationships could for the most part be avoided with something like this; "Hey _____ (fill in the blank: spouse, co worker, friend, etc.) I assume you either were unaware of your impact on me or didn't mean to impact me this way, but your action when you _____ (fill in the blank) was _____ (fill in the blank: hurtful, bothersome, etc.). I wanted to get that out in the open so it didn't fester and cause a division between us."

The Bible talks about this. It tells us to go to our brother or sister if there is a problem between the two of you (see Matthew 18).

The counseling world talks about this. It's called healthy conflict.

Seems so easy to do when I type it on my computer, read it in the Bible or hear it from a counselor.

Actually carrying out what is typed, read or heard – much harder.

And noble.

Had we made the bet on whether or not you too are an incognito chicken would you owe me $3?

If so, work to change that.

You can do a lot with $3.

Inspired
by Jared Caron

Who needs to be inspired?

We all need to be inspired. For me I need this in many moments of the day, week and month!

I often look to a pastor, a book, a story on the news, which can all be helpful.

I don't know about you but I need everlasting inspiration the kind that you can only find on the cross!

Have you ever had a moment in life where you could believe nothing but the truth of the cross, which is, Jesus died for us, and that was the only thing that would get you through that moment?

One of those moments for me was when they told us that our un-born child would have downs syndrome only 12 weeks into the pregnancy.

I rested in the cross that God would not give up on us

know matter what the outcome.

I would be able to handle anything that came our way.

I could rise to the occasion what ever it may be!

I was inspired by Jesus.

This is the inspiration that I need daily he is the inspiration that is everlasting in every moment and every breath.

God saw that Cody, my son, was a normal healthy little boy, however we were ready for anything because of the inspiration the cross has given us!

When was the last time you were inspired by Jesus?

Barf

by Rob Link

Barkly barfed.

We woke up to a putrid pile of puppy puke.

Needless to say it was a nasty way to start the day. You know this I'm sure. If you have or have had a dog at one point or another you've had to deal with such unholy hurl. What made it worse for us is that Barkly weighs 175 pounds. So when he heaves, he heaves in massive quantities.

After a little sleuthing we discovered that one of the kids had left a bowl of chili downstairs in front of the TV on the floor. Barkly thought it was a friendly offering just for him and woofed down the beany bowl of soon to be barf. The problem is that we Links like our chili spicy hot (there is no other way to have it) and Barkly's stomach likes chili mild – real mild.

It was the making of a perfect storm – a gastro intestinal nightmare.

If you are still reading you are either male (guys like vomit vernacular) and thus happy as a clam or you are really hoping this regaling of regurgitation is leading us somewhere.

It is.

What do we learn from my canine companion's digestive distress?

We learn that what goes in comes out.

What goes in…

…Comes out.

We are products of our consumption.

Certainly this applies to the food and drink we consume, but that isn't what I'm talking about.

I'm talking about the stuff we put in our hearts and minds. I'm talking about the stuff we watch, listen to, and ponder.

If we only watch negative things let's not be surprised if negativity seeps out.

If we only listen to angry things let's not be shocked when

anger becomes our companion.

If we only think morose and dark things lets not be stunned when our moods are morose and dark.

What goes in comes out.

If you are a dog named, Barkly, spicy chili goes in, spicy chili comes out.

If you are a human named Tom, Dick, or Harry, ickiness goes in, ickiness comes out.

If you are a human name Betty, Sally, or Sue, goodness goes in, goodness comes out.

What goes in comes out.

If you are at all in a reflective mood, what are you allowing in?

If you are not in a reflective mood you can ignore that last sentence and just go about your day.

The Gift of Ears
by Rob Link

I get exhausted each Wednesday during the winter.

At 4:30 each Wednesday afternoon I leave the house having swapped my four seat Honda Element for Kristy's seven seat Honda Odyssey and make the rounds picking up six 6th grade boys to take them to our practice where we meet the other two guys on the team.

For an hour I have the privilege of teaching these young fellas about the game of basketball. I teach them that defense and rebounds win basketball games. I teach them that turnovers loose basketball games. We start each week sharing high's and low's because a connected team is a better team. I teach them how to dribble and tell them that God gave them two hands so they could go right or left. "You've got two hands," I often yell, "use them both!" I teach them about focus and not whining about calls made or not made. I coach them to get in the lane and either shoot or kick it. I tell them that as long as they are in range and moderately open there is no bad shot. I teach them how to jump the ball and how to bring pressure full court. I tell them that defensive pressure is supposed to make the other team panic. I tell them that we don't need to panic if there is defensive pressure – three dribbles backward is a good thing. I teach them to not go for steals when they are on the ball but to go for every steal when they are off the ball by jumping passing lanes.

For an hour I am blowing my whistle, running up and down the court, teaching drills, showing stances, modeling right position, encouraging the discouraged, affirming the positive, correcting the negative and coaching at full volume.

And absolutely none of that tires me out. It's all rather invigorating to tell the truth.

Yet by the time I get home I am utterly exhausted.

"Why is that?" you ask. I'll tell you.

It's the car ride to and from that tuckers me out.

Six kids all vying to be heard and not a single one listening.

Not a single one listening.

As soon as one of the guys takes a breath while talking

there are five others jumping in and interrupting with a story that is bigger and better.

If you want to keep the discussion floor you better not pause for breath or mix in a comma. If you do, it's over.

Each week I want to scream "Quiet! You are stepping on his comma! Let him finish!"

At first, as I thought about this lack of listening, I chalked it up to pubescent posturing. But as the season has progressed I've seen more and more that this phenomenon is actually rampart across all age groups – my team only alerted me to its presence.

Nobody listens to anybody!

OK that might be a bit much. I get that it is a little hyperbolic. But not by much.

Think about it.

Watch and see.

Answer these questions:

How often are you preparing your story or statement while

the person you are with is talking?

How often have you had your comma stepped on?

How often have you stepped on someone's comma?

How often have you jumped in with your own story?

How often has someone asked you a question simply to learn more?

How often have you asked a question simply to learn more?

How often have you felt like someone was 100% interested in you and not using your story as a springboard to tell their own?

How often have you been 100% interested in someone not using their story as a springboard to tell your own?

We, in large part, are like a van full of 6th grade boys. Everybody's talking.

Nobody's listening.

God gave us two hands so we could drive right or left.

He gave us two ears so we could listen more than we speak.

Listen.

More than we speak.

When you listen to someone, really listen, you are blessing them with a gift.

You have a gift to give.

Give it.

Fear

by Brent Resh

In the Bible we see the word "fear" and "afraid" used often. Sometimes these words seem to be positive and other times negative.

The dictionary says that fear can mean "to highly respect" someone or it can mean "to be afraid of" someone.

There are many stories of people in the Bible who are afraid or full of fear. Adam and Eve were afraid after they ate the fruit (Genesis 3:10). Abraham was afraid that he would be killed because of his beautiful wife Sarah (Genesis 12:11). Moses was afraid after he killed the Egyptian (Exodus 2:14).

These stories are examples of people who had a bad kind of fear. Adam and Eve and Moses were afraid of the consequences of what they had done. They were fearful and scared of what was going to happen next. Adam and Eve hid, and Moses ran away. Abraham lied because he was afraid for his own safety. He didn't trust that God would protect him.

In these three stories, what might it have looked like if in each case, the characters had trusted God instead of making the choices they made?

> *And now, Israel, what does the Lord your God ask of you but to fear the Lord your God, to walk in obedience to him, to love him, to serve the Lord your God with all your heart and with all your soul, and to observe the Lord's commands and decrees that I am giving you today for your own good?*
> *Deuteronomy 10:12-13*

This is the other kind of fear – the good kind.

This is the kind of fear that comes from our reverence and respect for who God is.

So although it may seem strange, when we "fear" God we actually have nothing to be "afraid" of. When we live in fear of God, it means that we do our very best to obey and please him. When we live like that, God pours out his love and blessings on us.

David was a man who feared the Lord and was a man after God's own heart. Compare the story of David in 1 Samuel 17:34-45 to that of Abraham.

Think of a time when you were afraid. Did you pray or call out to God for help and how did you see God work?

Do you live like you fear God?

Lessons From Sochi
by Rob Link

I learned four things while watching the 2014 Winter Olympics.

1. I'm geographically illiterate. Kyrgyzstan and Tajikistan are countries? I had no idea. Didn't know they were countries and now that I do, I have no idea where they are.
2. Watching the moguls makes my knees ache. What type of crazy person would do that?
3. I'm old (ish). Most of the star athletes are half my age. Oh my.
4. I am made for significance and impact.

For our purposes today let's just focus on #4.

Something in me stirs almost to the point of tears (well ok to the point of tears a couple times), when I see these people who I have never met compete in an event I will never compete in to win a prize I'm really not interested in.

Moved to tears.

Over some people I don't know.

Doing a thing I will never do.

To win something I could care less about.

Why?

Because watching the Olympics awakens within me the reality that God has made me for greatness.

He made me to do something memorable.

He made me for impact. Lasting impact.

The kind that changes the world.

And here is a little secret…

He made you for greatness too.

It's true.

Pause and ask yourself:

Have you ever wondered why you get drawn into the Olympics or other sporting events?

Or if not the Olympics, movies like Braveheart*?*

Or if not movies like Braveheart, *stories like the one where that woman did that really awesome thing? (You see what I did there? I was vague so you could fill in your own story. Very clever isn't it?)*

Stories of overcoming and greatness touch something deep within.

Why do you think *The Hunger Games* and *The Hobbit* made $158 million and $190 million on their respective opening weekends?

Why do you think the super hero movies are always some of the top grossing films of our times?

Why do you think millions of people saw *Hansel and Gretel: Witch Hunters*? Oh wait, that didn't happen because it was a horrible movie.

Why do you think *Avatar* is the highest grossing movie of all times?

Because we are drawn to greatness. The heroes of all these movies accomplished great things in the face of seemingly insurmountable odds.

In our own way, that is what we want with our lives.

Overcoming obstacles and doing something great!

This is what Jesus was getting at when he said he chose us and appointed us to bear fruit, fruit that lasts!

That's simply Bible talk saying Jesus chose us to do awesome things! Things that will last well past our lifetimes!

I want you to know that you were not created for a life of ho hum existence. You were not created to merely get through life.

You were made to change the world. Or at least your little corner of it.

Ask yourself these two questions:

1. What change does your world need?
2. What change can you bring?

And then go overcome some obstacles and be great!

Poison ivy
by Dori Beltz

Have you ever had poison ivy?

I have it right now and I'm fighting the urge to scratch my leg completely off.

So crazy itchy.

I've traced the source of the poison ivy to a recent walk…it was a peace-filled morning stroll through the woods, my #1 place to "get with Jesus".

Where's your favorite place to spend time with Him?

My day started with some sweet Jesus time and was interrupted by a nasty little 3-leafed nightmare. Rude.

Just like the father of rudeness, aka Satan, the poison ivy tried to steal my joy. He's a sneaky devil. Always trying to disrupt my attempts to grow closer to God.

Check out Romans 7:21,

"It happens so regularly that it's predictable. The moment I decide to do good, sin is there to trip me up."

What trips you up?

God is way stronger than Satan and his annoying snares.

God is worth pursuing. God is worthy of our perseverance.

In the end, He dominates as our great Healer and provides relief from the itchiest of distractions. Keep seeking Him!

Top 10 Reasons to Pray
by Rob Link

1. It increases peace. Peace is good.
2. You have to deal with knuckleheads. Enough said.
3. Prayer diminishes the draw of temptation.
4. When you pray, you grow in wisdom. Can't ever have too much of that.
5. It connects you with the Creator, Redeemer, and Sustainer of the World!
6. You get to use words like "thee" and "thou." (But only if you want, you don't have to. I never do, but my childhood pastor, Pastor Max, did when I was a kid and he sounded awesome.)
7. Clarity of purpose and direction increases. This is good cause you get confused don't you?
8. At times life stinks, prayer helps.
9. At times life is awesome, prayer helps.
10. You get grumpy. Prayer whips grumpy into shape.

And one more, free of charge…

11. Prayer impacts the lives of those you pray for.

Blue is Dead
by Brian Fraaza

The other day, I took my daughter Maddy to the pet store. We looked at all the animals.

We started with the small rodents and moved on to the birds and lizards. Eventually we made our way back to the fish. We looked at all of them. From the goldfish to the glow-in-the-dark tropical ones to the flesh-eating carnivorous ones. We observed, studied and critiqued them all. Eventually we happened upon the pretty, colorful betas in their individual little bowls. There was one fish in particular, a blue one, that Maddy seemed particularly fond of…Every kid needs a pet, right?

And anyway…it could have been a lot worse. I could have come home with a bird or one of those creepy ferrets. But as it was, we left with a blue beta, a bowl and all of the other necessary accessories. We got home and set it all up and I asked Maddy what she wanted to name her fish. She said 'Blue.'

It would have been tough to argue the logic, so Blue it was. She loves Blue. He's the first thing she greets in the morning and the last creature she kisses goodnight. It makes me happy.

Today though is a sad day.

Blue is dead.

Maddy doesn't know this yet (please don't tell her). I know Maddy will be sad. Not so much because of Blue's death (as a four-year-old, I don't think she'll understand quite what that means) but just because her friend is absent.

I love my daughter and because I place a very high value on her happiness, I'm already making plans to purchase Blue's replacement, and I'm confident that she will never know the difference.

All this got me to thinking about God as my dad and how much he loves to bless me (and you). If it brings me such delight to watch Maddy trying to kiss Blue goodnight ("Honey, you can't put your head in the bowl"), how much joy does it bring God to watch us enjoy the gifts that he's given?

Check out Luke 11:11. What do you think about that?

Skin-tight just doesn't seem right
by Rob Link

Skin-tight just doesn't seem right.

The thought came to me a bit ago while running on the treadmill at the gym. Everywhere I looked there was a woman clad in skin-tight attire.

Everywhere.

My optical options were limited.

Option A: Get an eye full of womanly anatomy.

Option B: Keep my eyes shut.

Now here comes the delicate part. I've heard church folks rage against such things before. They have always seemed angry, condescending, and inflammatory. I've heard preachers rant against "Jezebel." I've read many an author who deride "Delilah." (FYI – they are two women of ill repute mentioned in the Bible.)

So before I go any further I want to distance myself in this discussion from such ranters and ragers.

I want to distance myself from them.

And I want you to know it.

First let me say to all women I am sorry. I am sorry for the stupidity of men who have perpetuated the lie that a woman is only as valuable as her shape. That is stupid, wrong, and damaging. I am sorry for the fact that men perpetuate the porn industry. I am sorry that men leer. I am sorry that men joke coarsely about females. I'm sorry for all the dishonoring-to-women-talk I've ever heard in the countless locker rooms I have found myself in. I'm sorry how high school boys talk of their "conquests" (most of them imaginary). I'm sorry older fellas behave like dirty old men.

Women I am sorry how the male species has let you down time and time again.

Secondly I want to give you a quick look into the mind of some of us men who do not want to see skin-tight everywhere we look. Whereas the female form is beautiful and enticing to look at, some of us (for a variety of reasons) would rather reserve our eyes for our wife's form only. It feels dishonoring to my wife to have multiple eye-fulls of other women in couldn't-be-tighter clothing.

Some of us want to walk biblically; "I made a vow to not look at a woman lustfully" and "If you even look at a woman lustfully you have already committed adultery in your heart."

Abstinence of the eye is a faith issue for many men.

Certainly the onus of responsibility for this falls on us. Yet skin-tight everywhere makes the task much more difficult.

Hopefully having distanced myself from the ranters and ragers, I want to lay out three reasons why skin-tight doesn't seem right:

1. It seems to be a subtle cat-fight between women. There seems to be an indirect competition to see whose form "wins." Not good for a variety of reasons. Here's two. It perpetuates the nonsense that a woman's shape is where she finds worth and it hinders healthy female to female relationships
2. If you as a woman feel affirmed by the lingering looks of a man know this; the man who is leering at you isn't only leering at you. He is most likely leering at all the ladies. In his brokenness he relegates women

to the level of inanimate object like a sports car that is impersonally oogled as if it could be used simply for his pleasure and his pleasure alone. And then discarded.
3. As mentioned above, skin-tight makes abstinence of the eyes difficult for those of us who strive for such a thing.

Having said all that, I want to ask something from the female readers.

Of course you are free to say no.

I want to ask all women reading this to explore modesty like you have never explored it before.

Research the topic. Have discussions. Seek greater understanding. If you are a person of biblical faith see what the Bible has to say about the subject.

And then, after having mulled over the matter, act upon what you have discovered.

Checking Out
by Anna Joy Tucker

I've stopped looking at the magazine covers in the grocery store check out aisle.

Instead, I look at the candy bars, the gum, or the "incentive items", which apparently you buy only because you see them, not because you need them or even previously knew they existed.

I'll look at that stuff, sure. But no magazine covers.

Some of it is to avoid falling into the comparison trap, spending the next couple of weeks trying to talk myself into being okay with the body I currently occupy.

Some of it is to rebel against the constant push for perfection. "How to own the best wardrobe on your block!" "Beauty miracles that will make *everyone* jealous." "16 secrets of having photogenic arms…" and so on.

Mostly, though, I've stopped looking at magazine covers in an effort to stop lusting.

Yep.

Lusting.

You know, that ugly word that gets tossed around in Christian school assemblies and men's Bible studies and youth group lock in parties, late at night when things have turned from silly to serious.

Usually, "lusting" means having sexual thoughts about someone who is not your spouse.   Usually, "lusting" means "wanting" in a sexual way. Usually, "lusting" is something that mostly men struggle with.

Or so we're told.

Here's the truth.

I don't struggle with sexual thoughts about the women plastered across the shelves. I don't try to picture them naked or imagine scenarios with them and me. I don't "want" them. But I do want what they *have*.

I lust for their power.

I lust for their sexiness.

I lust for their perfection.

I want to be the most desirable woman in a room. I want to be the one turning the heads. Sometimes, even, the husband heads. I want the attention and the admiration. I want to prance around like I imagine the magazine women do, perfectly content with my every inch, never once having a doubt or a question about my beauty and my acceptability.

That's what I lust for.

And I know some ways to get it.

I know that if I wear certain things and speak in certain tones and stand in certain positions, I will get attention. I will get eyes and heads glued to me.

That's the truth.

But here's the secret.

The eyes and heads that watch me are also watching many, many others. The eyes and heads that watch me were made to only watch the one they are meant to pair up with for life.

You see, the entire notion of perfection, of desirability, of sexiness, has been tampered with, and I want to see us get back to the root. Back to the truth.

The truth is that there is no such thing as ultimate perfection. There is no such thing as being the *most* desirable one. All of the promises that we are fed about what our body must look like and what we must wear and how we must present ourselves are based in an idea that we can follow these rules and become the god. We can become the *one* who is worthy of attention and desire.

The truth is that instead of exposing myself to everyone, in an effort to be wanted by everyone, I must believe and operate in the truth that I was already made to be wanted by One.

I was not made to draw attention to myself. I was made to draw attention to Jesus. And I was made to get attention by Him.

I have been lied to and made to believe that if I appear a certain way, I will get the attention I seek. And it will all be for me. And it will make me happy and whole.

I don't know about you. But following that lie and living under the rules that come with it is exhausting and impossible. It never brings peace and happiness. It brings obsession and naval-gazing.

Instead, I want to learn the truth. I want to let the truth do what it does best. Set me free.

I don't want to lust for power.

I don't want to lust for perfection.

Instead, I choose to prance around my life, perfectly content with my every inch, never once having a doubt or a question about my beauty and my acceptability.

Because I am *seen* and *known* and *loved* by the One who fills all the desires.

How about you?

Want to come along?

Don't be mean
by Rob Link

I've been told I look like a drug dealer.

I've been told that I'm leading people to hell.

I've been told that I work for Satan.

I've been told I was useless.

I've been yelled at, sworn at, scoffed at, and scorned.

I've been ridiculed for my clothing and dismissed for my appearance.

This is some damaging crap.

I'm not sharing for sympathy. I'm really not.

A great wife, some good friends, and a helpful therapist have me in a place where I can say, "I'm doing well in spite of all that junk."

No, I'm not sharing for sympathy. I'm sharing to make a

point.

Here's the point: all of those things have come my way from Christians.

Yikes.

"Be kind and compassionate to one another," says the Bible.

The church has often struck out on this one.

I'm not the only one who has had hurtful things thrown my way from The Church or a Christian.

Some of you have your own list.

Here's the point: If you are a follower of Jesus you ought to lead the kindness charge.

Here's the point: Don't be mean.

What mean things have you heard?

Have you processed them with some friends so they don't haunt you? If not you might want to do so soon?

What mean things have you said?

Who have you hurt?

Go apologize if necessary.

Free Breakfast
by Rob Link

A while back Taco Bell was giving away free breakfast to anyone who walked through their doors.

My family went nuts.

My oldest, Jake, went on multiple occasions during the week and brought friends with him.

Kristy went twice – in one day! She took the Max and Zeke early before school, dropped them off, went home, got Reese and Elyse, and went right back.

The girls were so excited they had to share the yummy goodness with their favorite custodian at their elementary school. They brought him a free Taco Bell breakfast.

He was happy.

Some things will do that to you. Make you happy.

So happy in fact that you can't help but revel in the goodness and share the joy with others.

Some things will do that to you. Like free food.

Jesus is better than free food.

Sometimes we Christians get it wrong and think our faith is angry or grumpy or condescending. Then we act accordingly: angry, grumpy or condescending.

Yet it's good news. Really good news.

Did you know that the word Gospel (a word used to describe the news of Jesus) literally means "good news?"

Did you know that the Bible says that God loved the world (yes the whole world) so much that he sent his son Jesus so that whoever would believe in him would have eternal life? Did you know this?

Did you know that the Bible says that God didn't send his son into the world to condemn the world but to save it? Awesome!

Did you know the Bible says that God desires for none to perish, but for all to be saved? Did you know?

Yes, this is good news.

Better than free breakfast.

Tell someone this week about this good news.

Recurring Dream
by Rob Link

The other night I had a recurring dream. It's a dream that I have at least 3 or 4 times a month.

In my dream, I am young of body and able to jump really high. I am usually playing basketball of course (the game of heaven) and dunking on everybody.

Then I wake up.

Bummer.

My first thought is, "crap, I want to go back to that dream." And I try to do just that. I squint my eyes really tight and try very hard to get back to high flying bliss.

But alas I never can. I'm left with the reality of multiple sports injuries and a body that has to walk around the pile of dog poo in the back yard cause I can't jump over it!

As I said, bummer.

Here's the deal – too many folks waste their lives trying to live in the glory of dreams gone by.

I'll say that again. Too many folks waste their lives trying to live in the glory of dreams gone by.

Although common, this is silly.

God says, "I know the plans I have for you…"

Future plans. For tomorrow. Plans to hope for. Plans that say more is coming. Good stuff on the way.

So don't waste your life dreaming of yesterday's glory.

Live today. In this moment. With hope of good things to come.

What recurring dreams do you have?

How can you "live in the moment?"

Wrecking Ball
by Rob Link

I realized that Miley Cyrus and I have two things in common.

No, I have never ridden naked on a wrecking ball so get that out of your mind.

What do we have in common?

We both used to have a lot more hair.

And… we both have the propensity to enter a situation riding the proverbial wrecking ball – metaphorically speaking.

It's the second thing that I would like to ponder a bit (not much to ponder about my defeat to male pattern baldness).

A wrecking ball is used on things that are meant to be demolished – never to be rebuilt. Knocked down. Destroyed. Irreparably altered.

Here's some truth: A wrecking ball has no place within relationships.

None.

Yet careless words, inattention to tone, ill placed hyperbole (like in an argument), and volatile verbiage knock down the walls of any relationship faster than a wrecking ball knocks down an old building.

How do I know this? Cause I'm guilty.

My careless words, inattention to tone, ill placed hyperbole (like in an argument), and volatile verbiage have hurt people.

Most of the time (I think) the hurt I've caused has been unintentional. Yet damage is done whether intent is there or not.

How about you?

Have you heard your tone is hurtful?

Are your words are damaging?

Do you fight dirty in a "discussion?"

Are you often shocked that you have been hurtful?

If so I have 2 things to say to you:
   1. Ignorance is no excuse.
   2. Saying, "I didn't mean too" doesn't make it ok.

Are you like Miley and me? If so I have 2 assignments for you:
   1. Go apologize.
   2. Work your butt off to get off the wrecking ball.

Barkly is a Glutton
by Rob Link

My dog has no self-control.

None what so ever.

Kristy went shopping the other day. As soon as she got all the groceries into the house she had to run out and pick up the girls from school.

When she and the girls came in, there was Barkly, with a silly, happy grin on his face and three (yes I said three) empty bagel bags.

Note I didn't say three bagels. I said three *bags* of bagels. Each bag had eight within. Let me do the math for you. My pooch ate 24 bagels in the span of ten minutes.

24 bagels! One dog!

He should be embarrassed at his overt lack of self-control. 24 bagels. My goodness. (For the record, he once at a whole pan of lasagna single handedly, uh..., I mean single pawedly.)

Barkly isn't the only one I know who lacks self-control. In fact dogs aren't the only species to exhibit such a trait. We humans are pretty good at it too.

A lack of self-control has two buddies: Overindulgence and self-neglect.

I'm not trying to over dramatize things here. It's true when I say these three have caused all kinds of harm. From low self esteem to heart attacks. From anger to broken relationships. From obesity to insomnia. And this is only the tip of the ice burg!

All can come from a lack of self-control and it's two accompanying pals.

Here's the dreaded question:

Do you lack self-control? (It's dreaded not because the answer is hard to find. No, the answer is easy to see, but difficult to admit – thus dreaded.)

Here's a comforting truth – most of us do. You're not a freak if you find such a lack in your life. Just normal. And in need of a change.

So what do you think?

Is time to make some changes?

Ask a friend and begin the journey together.

Trust me, you don't want to live the rest of your life like a Newfoundland in a room full of bagels. There is too much crap (you should have seen what Barkly did in the backyard afterward) to deal with when you live without self-control.

Stinky Apologies
by Rob Link

Here's one thing I've learned about people (myself included for I am a people):

We are naturally horrible at apologies.

That's a bummer. Because in this life we will need to do some apologizin' since none of us is perfect.

In general we screw it up in one of two ways.

1. We mope, gush sorrow and excessive remorse, and apologize with such guilt and shame that the apology really becomes about how awful we feel and not the apology itself. And thus the offended party gets lost in the mix. This, my friends is a stinky apology.
2. Or we give a pseudo apology. "I'm sorry *you* felt that way" or "I'm sorry *if* you were hurt" or "I'm sorry, *but if you wouldn't have…*" or "*If* I might have done something that *you* might have not liked…". This type of deflecting and justifying also waters down the apology. It says to the one who is receiving the apology, "I'm not going to own my mistake, you are

too sensitive and for that I'm sorry." And thus the offended party gets lost in the mix. This, my friends is a stinky apology.

Let me offer a bit of counsel on the topic.

Three easy steps. Nine short words. Eleven syllables:

1. "I'm sorry."
2. "I was wrong."
3. "Can you forgive me?"

That's it.

Don't load your own shame into the mix. Don't add "if-you-would've's." Don't make excuses. Take responsibility.

That's it. Short and simple.

If you feel this is unnatural and wonder if you could ever apologize in such a way, don't worry. You will have ample opportunity to practice.

Lest the thought of your future failures lead you to go away miserable – don't. The fact that you will fail just makes you human – a human who needs to apologize and not an evil, unworthy of life human.

Relax. Cut yourself some slack. And learn to apologize well.

Where do you need to enact this 9 word apology strategy?

Impact
by Rob Link

She blessed me a ton.

Because of her I have had the blessing of: rich friendship – the type that changes a life for the better, godly counsel in the midst of countless confusing conundrums, laughter beyond measure, joy in the midst of my dark days of depression, accountability and support that helped me stay free from my stupidity. Without a doubt, she blessed me a ton.

And I only met here a few times before she died. I really didn't know her that well.

Yet there is no doubt she blessed me a ton.

How can that be if I really didn't know her?

She was the mom of one of my closest friends. She shaped him and molded him into the man that he is today. He knows how to bring light to dark places – because of her. He knows how to bring peace where there is chaos – because of her. He brings wisdom in the midst of confusion – because of her. He brings joy to sad places – because of her. He makes people laugh – because of her. He spreads the love of Jesus – because of her.   He has made my life better – because of her.

Seems to me that one of the marks of a great life is touching the lives of people you don't know.

Do you "know" someone like this woman who blessed me?

Humbled
by Rob Link

A while back I attended a pastors chapel at a local Christian Elementary School.

I usually hate such gatherings.

Posing, preening pastors mingling awkwardly with cups of crappy coffee clasped in hand. It sort of reminds me of the peacocks at the zoo who try to out feather-flaunt their fellow fowls. I walk around feeling a bit like a fish out of water.

Quite frankly most of the other pastors bug me. It's not uncommon for me to begin ticking off a list of all of their faults. I see them and make mental judgments as to why their churches are probably shrinking.

Not my favorite environment. As I said, I usually hate such gatherings.

I say "usually" because on this particular occasion I loved it.

During the festivities I had the privilege of sitting next to this precious little kindergartener who I've known since she was born. I see her most every Sunday at church. For 45 minutes we sat side by side sharing laughs and giggles. We had a lot of fun. There were times when we were surrounded by a bunch of other kids who go to our church, but she was my constant companion. She made the morning highly enjoyable.

As the service wound its way down, she turned to me with her big puppy dog eyes. I could tell she was working up the courage to say something to me. I thought, "For sure she will tell me I made her morning or what an awesome pastor I was. She will probably tell me in her kindergarten way that she feels fortunate to be a part of our church."

After having spent most an hour with me she asked, "Who are you?"

She had no clue who I was. To her I was just another posing, preening pastor. I couldn't help but laugh.

Humorously humbled.

As needed.

At just the right time.

In a perfect way.

By a kid.

Her question reminded me that I could have been a blessing to the other pastors. Instead I was an aloof idiot. I missed an opportunity.

Someday I won't need these lessons. Someday I will be free from my own stupidity.

Until then, I'm thankful God uses "the mouth of babes" to teach me.

When have you had similar arrogant, condescending thoughts (I know you've had them)?

How were you humbled?

Take a minute to thank God for such lessons.

Crazy Parents
by Rob Link

Max had a basketball tournament.

There are some crazy parents out there.

One lady when her son was slightly bumped (and got the foul call) screamed at the top of her lungs "He's choking my baby! He's choking my baby!" For crying out loud it was only an accidental bump, and her "baby" was a 6'2" 190lb man-child.

This dad I saw must have had super powers. He was all the way across the gym with his view blocked by several players, and yet he clearly saw a foul that the ref who was a mere two feet away missed entirely. Amazing. Of course this dad let the whole world know of his herculean vision by vociferously proclaiming the aforementioned ref's ineptitude and blindness.

Another dad, beat so loudly on the bleachers for the whole game as if they were bongos in need of discipline that everyone left and went and sat on the other side of the gym. I asked him if he played drums. He said, "Not anymore, I just want my son to hear my support." My goodness, the neighboring county heard his support.

One mom who had driven all the way from Ohio to cheer on her son simply howled like a wolf every time her son touched the ball. Loudly. Very loudly.

There are some crazy parents out there.

Their antics were nutty, ill informed, a bit hysterical, and all together harmless.

And enjoyable to behold. I liked them.

I liked them because it was evidence that these crazy parents were crazy for their kids.

I liked them because it was the reflection of God in those crazy parents. The Bible tells us we are all created in his image and at times show some god-like qualities – like being crazy about our kids.

You probably know that the Bible refers to God as Father many many times. Did you know that he is also compared to a "mother hen" who longs to draw her chicks to herself? Did you know that he is compared to a nursing mother who cannot forget her nursing child?

God is likened to a father, a mother hen, and a nursing mom.

God is a parent.

And he is crazy for you and me – his kids.

He's as crazy for us as any nutty basketball parent is for their kid.

More so.

What crazy-parent-moments have you seen?

Do you know God is crazy about you?

Fear of Bikes
by Rob Link

I was watching Elyse (our 6 years old) ride her bike the other day. It made me think back to my early bike riding days.

I didn't learn until I was in fourth grade.

Fourth grade!

Before I ever gained my bicycle balance my buddies and brother, Jason, were riding wheelies and jumping curbs. They had all learned much earlier than I.

My tardiness to the pedal cost me countless trips to the neighborhood candy store. I sadly watched them pedal their way to sweet sugary heaven unable to ride along and to slow afoot to keep up with them.

While Jason and my pals were riding to and from school in liberated bliss, I was stuck riding the bus.

Alone.

In sadness.

I missed out on a ton.

What was it that kept me off the bike for so long? I remember very clearly.

Fear.

I was scared to death of falling, crashing, scraping, tumbling, and bleeding. So scared that I avoided the bike as if it were a rat infected with the bubonic plague. I was sure the moment I straddled the bike it would throw me off just like an enraged bull throws those crazy cowboys. There was no way I was going to go the way of the bucked-off-buckaroo! My own two feet were good enough and really, how bad was the bus anyway?

Yet I realized that at some point or another we all must face our fears. I didn't want to be an old man who had no bike riding memories to reflect upon in his dotage.

So on some random day in the fourth grade I said enough is enough. I asked my dad to take my bike and me to an open parking lot.

With fear and trepidation I mounted my un trusty stead,

put my pro keds to the pedal and immediately rode smack dab into the broad side of my dads truck – which happened to be the only vehicle in the whole accursed parking lot!

My fear became reality.

Crashed.

Bloodied.

And yet still alive.

Quite fine in fact.

The crash didn't hurt and the blood felt like my own little red badge of courage.

I encountered that which I feared and yet I would still live? Amazing! What Joy! My fears had been ill founded. Shock of all shocks. Crashing and bleeding was not the end of the world!

The fear that had crippled me amounted to nothing when it was faced.

Let me say that again. The fear that had crippled me

amounted to nothing when faced.

I got back up, mounted my now trusty two-wheeled stead and rode like a champ.

What fears do you have?

What are they keeping you from?

Thoughts on Church and Bathrobes
by Rob Link

I remember growing up thinking two things about church:

1. I loved the God that is talked about at church.
2. Church must be for the ladies and not the fellas.

I came to the 2nd conclusion because I saw men standing around awkwardly at church while the women were thoroughly engaged. Although the pastor was always male, all the active members were female. And the dude who was the pastor always wore this thing that looked like a bathrobe!

Yikes. "What type of man wears a robe to work," I wondered. No other man in any other place I observed. So the answer to my wondering was, "a godly man of course."

To be a godly man one must wear a robe to work.

A bathrobe.

To work.

Yuck. As a young boy who only saw women involved in the church (a church which was led by a fella wearing a bathrobe!) I concluded that although I loved God, the church was not for me. To be godly must only be for the female species and the rare man who wears bathrobes to work.

Yet as my understanding of things Bible increased I began to see that my earlier conclusion was wrong.

Check these facts out:

1. David was a godly man and he kicked a@#!
2. Samson was one bad dude who did awesome guy things to save God's people.
3. Ehud was a left handed swordsmen who whupped a chubby king so that the people of God might walk into freedom
4. Jesus himself got angry at the folks who were exploiting the poor at the temple and went nuts.

It really doesn't take long to see these four stories aren't exceptions, but the norm.

Nor does it take long for me to realize that the lack of "maleness" at my childhood church was not by biblical design but rather by unintentional human consequence.

There is more to this Christian faith than dudes who were robes, awkward men, and overly involved females! Upon further review there is something very appealing to the male species.

And now, in spite of my childhood thoughts, I am a pastor.

As a pastor, here are two things I want:

1. I want to reintroduce men to the awesomeness of church and the Jesus behind it.
2. I want to never, never, never wear a bathrobe while preaching.

What memories, if any, do you have of your childhood church?

How were men involved in the church?

What misconceptions did/do you have about the role of gender in the church?

Mean or stupid
by Rob Link

There is a difference between malicious and ignorant.

This is a helpful distinction to grasp as we walk through life. Here's why – people are going to let us down, hurt us, disappoint us, and fail us time and time again. (Just like we will them.)

Most of the time the offense/failure is a matter of ignorance and not maliciousness.

And that makes a world of difference.

When we think someone did that thing intentionally with the goal to hurt us – the hurt runs deeper.

If we think that someone did that exact same thing that hurt us out of stupidity, it hurts less.

It is a matter of intent.

Evil vs. fallible.

Intentional vs. mistake.

Malicious vs. ignorance.

At times people will be intentionally malicious – but not most of the time. Most of the time it is a matter of ignorance.

Yet it seems we assume most of our hurts are done maliciously and only a few are a result of ignorance.

Life might be freer if we switch up our assumptions.

When was the last time you hurt someone?

Was it intentionally malicious or unintentionally stupid?

When was the last time you were hurt?

Was it intentionally malicious or unintentionally stupid?

Pride Before...
by Rob Link

Jake's high school basketball team, Loy Norrix High School, was playing in a tournament. They did pretty good, beating some teams they were not expected to beat.

Before one such game the other team was rather boisterously proclaiming their victory pre-tip.

"Let's hurry up and get this quick win."

"They're all scrubs."

"This will be easy."

The ball went up, Loy Norrix showed up, trash talking mouths shut up, and the prideful got beat up.

Hmmm... Seems to me the Bible says something about pride going before a fall.

A great lesson.

Humility beats pride.

What grade would you give yourself in regard to humility?

Ask someone who knows and loves you to give you a grade.

How do the two grades compare?

Blind Spot
by Rob Link

It used to be when men wanted to disguise their losing battle to male pattern baldness they went with the comb-over. Windy days were the bane of every such mans existence.

As one who has lost the battle to the aforementioned dreaded disease, I'm going to let you in on a secret. Here it is:

The shaved head is today's comb-over. Most of us who shave our heads want you to believe we shave out of choice. In reality it is to hide the accursed (at least accursed in my self conscious opinion) horseshoe halo of hair. If I shave my head I can at least fool myself into thinking no one knows how bald I really am.

If you can't save it – shave it.

Crazy isn't it.

I've been enacting this deception for over 12 years now.

Over those 12 years I've learned something about shaving

the old noggin. I've learned that I am prone to miss the same spot right behind my ears if I am not careful. There have been many times I've been out and about only to discover a little unshaved spot right behind my ear. Never anywhere else. If I've missed a spot it is right there behind my flappers. It's my shaving blind spot I need to be extra careful with. When I shave my dome I need to be particularly mindful of that area.

Here's a parallel for you:

We have a similar thing when it comes to life.

You might not need to worry about shoplifting, but you need to be extra mindful of your propensity to get sinfully angry and harsh. You might not be tempted to murder your neighbor (depending on your neighbor), but you have a tendency to walk around with an arrogance so large your neck can't support the size of your head. You might not be prone to walk into adultery (or maybe you might) but you have a regular urge to walk in judgment and condemnation of anyone different than you.

What's your blind spot?

Ask a parent/friend what your blind spot is?

Might be a good idea to be particularly mindful of that area.

A Walk in the Woods
by Rob Link

My friend Rod and I took a few young men backpacking into the Smokey Mountains. Nothing but us, what we could carry on our backs and the great out doors for 3 nights and 4 glorious days.

Oh, and 28 miles, 6,000 feet of descent, and 6,000 feet of ascent.

If you have never trekked into the backcountry you will not know the joys of unadulterated nature nor will you know the mental assault that the miles and mountains make on your mind.

For some it is pure heaven.

For others it is pure hell.

We had one young man for whom the trip seemed closer to the later than the former. Let's call him George.

I knew he might struggle when a mere 50 yards into the hike he asked if we could take a break because he was tired. My thought at the time – "Uh Oh."

There were times when George thought he couldn't take another step let alone finish the grueling trip. At times he seemed broken with despair. It was physically demanding all he had to give and then some. At one point while crossing a knee-deep river, he slipped, flipped onto his backpack and submerged all of his stuff in the icy mountain water. My thought at the time – "Uh Oh."

Our last day included a 4,000 foot elevation gain over several miles. Needless to say we were all tuckered out – George more so than the rest of us. When we finally reached our vehicle George collapsed in fatigue. He was a puddle of tiredness and exhaustion.

He raised his head to speak. My thought at the time – "Uh Oh." I thought for sure he would launch into a complaining tirade.

Yet to my surprise, rather than making some disparaging remarks he said something incredibly profound.

"That was the most difficult thing I have ever done. And the best thing I have ever done."

Then he collapsed back into a semi catatonic heap.

Wow. What wisdom from a 14-year-old young man.

Out of difficult times come our best times.

So profound I'll say it again.

Out of difficult times come our best times.

I think we can learn something form George.

Often the best things in life are the most difficult.

What difficult situation(s) are you facing?

Go read the last 3 lines again.

The Sweet Nectar of Heaven
by Rob Link

She was counting her change as Barkly and I walked by.

It was Sunday morning, and the pooch and I were taking our half time walk (i.e. between services). We happened upon this woman we had seen in church who was hunched over her open palm filled with loose coins. It was clear she was counting the last of her monthly support. She'd have to wait until the first of the month to have any cash again. Until then she would rely on the Kalamazoo Gospel Mission to meet her basic needs.

She saw us coming, put her money away and walked with us. We struck up a conversation – nothing deep, simply light and casual. As I was turning right, she kept going straight and said, "Well, I'm off to buy a soda. See you next Sunday."

As we walked our separate ways, I said, "Good idea, a Mt. Dew sounds great right now."

About 25 minutes later Barkly and I made our way back to church where we stationed ourselves to greet the second service folks. One of our security guys came over with an ice-cold Mt. Dew saying some lady had dropped it off for me.

It was the same woman I had walked with earlier.

The same homeless woman who was down to her last penny.

The same woman who would have to wait two weeks before her next support check.

The same woman who was excited to buy herself a chilly beverage on a hot morning.

The very same woman.

And she spent her last dime on me!

In our home we jokingly yet affectionately call Mt. Dew, The Sweet Nectar of Heaven.

This time, there really was something heavenly about the dew.

What is your favorite soda?

How can you bless someone like this homeless woman blessed me?

Do You See
by Rob Link

Barkly and I were walking downtown.

Since one of us is rather striking and handsome we often get stopped by strangers who want to meet the good-looking one.

While walking this gentleman slowed down – I assumed to say hi to Barkly. Thinking he wanted to meet my fetching fury friend I stopped, made a moment of eye contact and said, "Hi."

His response surprised me. He wasn't stopping to greet to my hairy hound. He was stopping to say hi to me.

Unbeknownst to me he had been coming to The River the last few weeks having recently found himself homeless.

As I looked him in the eye and offered a greeting he said rather vehemently, "that's why I love The River!"

Wondering if he was referencing the handsome nature of the lead pastor and his dog, but not sure, I inquired as to what he was talking about.

"You guys see homeless people! I mean really see us! Most people walk right on by and never see us. You guys have made me feel apart of a family. Sometimes I feel like a ghost. Unseen."

Like a ghost.

Unseen.

My heart broke for this man and the homeless community.

At the same time I was inspired by my church that sees – really sees - homeless people while offering a place within the family.

Who do you not see?

Bouncing With Bobbie
by Rob Link

He is a bit awkward. He has the potential to make some folks uncomfortable.

And he likes to dance.

In church.

During the worship.

And well, there is no polite way to say this; he has never had dancing lessons. His dancing consists of bouncing. Just bouncing. Up and down as if he were on a pogo stick.

It is a good cardiovascular workout, but as I said, it is a bit awkward.
Awkward and beautiful.

Incredibly beautiful.

Bobbie was born with some rather pronounced cognitive impairments. His mind doesn't function "normally."

Thus he is free from the fear of what people think of him (at least during worship).

This is beautiful.

And enviable. How I wish I were as free from the tyranny of appearances.

His freedom is contagious. At times numerous people join him up front bouncing and dancing. Dancing and bouncing. Young and old alike join Bobbie in his unbridled worship, free of self-consciousness.

It was beautiful.

During worship, while most are standing I prefer to sit. Yet when Bobbie came over to me, grabbed my hands, and pulled me to my feet I had one thought,

"It's a good day to bounce."

So I stood up and bounced with Bobbie.

In what areas of your life would you like to be more like Bobbie?

Things I've Learned About Marriage
by Rob Link

Marriage Equals…

Marriage = Two souls set on a wonderful, God-ordained, cosmic collision course.

Marriage = Two good things (i.e. people) coming together to make something even better.

Marriage = Two wounded souls providing healing to one another.

Marriage = Two people made for joy finding joy in each other.

Marriage = Two individuals becoming one inseparable unit.

Marriage = Four eyes crying the same tears.

Marriage = Four feet walking one path.

Marriage = Two hearts breaking over the same things.

Marriage = Two hearts rejoicing over the same things.

Marriage = One refining tool.

Marriage = Two narcissists learning humility.

Marriage = Two beings living naked and unashamed (both literally and figuratively).

Marriage = One God's idea.

Marriage = Two sexual critters discovering sexual fulfillment – again and again and again...

Marriage = Two mouths laughing the same laugh.

Marriage = Two different people learning differences aren't better or worse – just different.

Marriage = Two crazy people acting as one to reflect God's image for the world to see.

Thoughts on Sex
by Rob Link

We were made to enjoy sex.

Lots of it.

Often.

Regularly.

Again.

And again.

And again.

With our spouse.

Within marriage.

In the beginning God said "Let the dude leave his parents" (just to be clear, the word "dude" is a paraphrase of the Biblical text), cleave to his wife, and the two shall become one flesh."

Here's the 3 step Biblical formula:

Step 1 – leave the home of your youth. Saying good-bye to mom and dad to start a home/family of your own.

Step 2 – Cleave. In the Old Testament language this cleaving was representative of a formal and binding ceremony, much akin to our wedding ceremonies today. During this ceremony in Old Testament times an animal or two was killed, some solemn words were spoke, some promises were made and then the two would be considered married.

Step 3 – Become one flesh. This is the sex act baby! Two becoming one flesh as they are joined in sexual union! The text also talks about the two being naked together and not ashamed. This is nothing other than Biblical license to be fully active sexually. Explore and exhaust one another in the marriage bed – it's God's plan.

Note that step 3 comes after step 2. The plan was for marriage then sex. Not the other way around.

Marriage.

Then sex.

In that order.

Here's what I tell my kids about sex, "It's awesome. It's one of your mothers and my favorite past times. (They hate that part of my sex talk.) You were made to enjoy sex. Someday you will be wonderfully sexually active. Save it for your spouse. You can wait. Your mom and I did. You are not a dog who must act on impulses. Wait. Marry. Then enjoy.

"Again.

"And again.

"And again."

If you are not married, I hope this inspires you to hang in there until you are. As a non-married person, what messages have you heard about sex?

As a married person what messages have you heard about sex?

Grandma turned 95
by Rob Link

We drove to New York to celebrate Grandma's 95th birthday.

The weekend before we had celebrated one of my kids 9th birthday. For my daughter the party was laced with gifts of all kinds.

Clothes, crafts, knick knacks and overly sweet snacks.

For her birthday there was a lot of stuff.

Every other kid at her party was jealous at the birthday bounty. And why wouldn't they be? Who doesn't like getting stuff?

I certainly do.

And I bet most of you do too.

After all, who doesn't like getting stuff?

Grandma doesn't, that's who.

For her birthday party she was explicit in her directions.

No presents, just people.   Family in particular.   That's it. Nothing more, nothing less. She has learned something after all those years.

Stuff doesn't matter as much as people.

Who, not what.

As her years wind down, she knows deep down in her soul that family and friends are much more valuable than things.

Who are the valuable people in your life?

If you haven't seen them in a while, get in touch and say, "hi, I love you and miss you."

Selfie
by Rob Link

Some facts about selfies:
- More than 17 million selfies are uploaded weekly.
- 33% of people with smart phones post at least once a week.
- 17% of the over 55 population regularly take a selfie, compared to 10% of 18-24 (wow, didn't see that coming! A higher percentage of the AARP crowd takes selfies – higher than the college crowd.)
- 36% say they alter their selfies (figure, eye color, skin tone, and lips are the top things altered)
- 34% of men who take selfies admit to altering their photos. Only 13% of women. (Are men just more honest??)
- The Selfie is the most popular genre of photography in the world.

When 2000 adults were asked, "How would you define people who take selfies?" the top answers were:

- Attention-seeking
- Vain
- Self absorbed

- Egotistical
- Insecure

Seems a bit harsh to me.

I wonder if the selfie craze is rooted in something deeper. I wonder if it is more than vain, egotistical attention seeking?

Could it be that the selfie phenomenon at its core is a longing for deep, authentic community?

I think so.

When God made Adam, He looked at him and said, "It is not good for the dude to be alone."

Not good to be alone.

We were made for community. Not the superficial, you-better-have-your-act-together type of community. No, I'm talking about the type of community where we are really known, really seen – warts and all – and still loved and accepted.

This type of community is rare. More often than not, our places of belonging are built around a false, inauthentic, everyone-looks-after-themselves-first mentality.

We live in a crowded world filled with lonely people.

Very few are truly seen, truly known. Most are subconsciously crying out, "Will someone see me?! Will someone love me?!"

Thus we have a selfie culture.

Who is in your close community?

A Thought on Christmas via Buddy
by Rob Link

Kristy and I were talking about *Elf* (the movie staring Will Farrell). In addition to the wonderful humor there is some deep truth kicking in the movie. I'm thinking of the scene when Buddy, employed by a department store as an elf, hears that Santa is coming to town. He goes nuts – yelling and screaming, "He's coming, he's coming!!!" On the surface it's a hilarious scene. Yet if you look at it with your God goggles on, you can see a lesson on the season of advent.

Advent is a time of preparation and waiting for the coming of the Messiah. For most of us Jesus gets lost amidst the gifts, traffic, credit card bills, parties, etc.

Buddy's single-minded excitement (for him it was only about seeing Santa, nothing else) is a great call for us to wonder what is keeping us from single-minded excitement about Jesus coming. The key for Buddy's intense jocularity was simply the fact that he knew – really knew – Santa and was known by him.

My prayer for myself and my family and for all of you is

that we would know Jesus – really know him and be fully known by him.

What does it mean to "know Jesus" like Buddy knew Santa?

Do you know Jesus like that?

Seven Days
by Rob Link

A while back I found myself hanging out with forty-four church planters in Phoenix at a training event. A great bunch of people. The event was called Thrive: Boot Camp for Church Planters. It was a weeklong training event that gave pastors the tools needed to start a new church. I had the privilege of speaking at the opening session.

If you've been around the River for any length of time you can probably guess what I told them was the most foundational tool needed for them to start a new fruitful church – intimacy with Jesus.

The average pastor prays less than 3 minutes a day – yikes.

For fruit, joy, and transformation we need to have praying pastors.

Since we believe all are called to ministry (only a few called to ministry within a church) that truth applies to all of you too. The way to a freer more complete and fruitful you is to be intimate with the Lord.

I asked these planters if they could commit to meeting in solitude with the Lord every day the rest of the week to read the word, pray and ask, worship, and listen for a half hour.

I want to ask you to do the same thing for a week. Can you do that? 7 days with Jesus. Give it a try and see how things are after the week is over.

It's Yours
by Wil Crooks

Some of my favorite things growing up were my bike, my bed, my baseball glove, and my Philadelphia Phillies long-sleeve T. The reason I liked these things so much was because they fit me just right. I could ride a friends' bike – but it was not as fast. I could sleep over at a friends' house, but I was always happy to get home and sleep in my own bed. I rarely could use my friends' baseball glove because I'm left handed. My friends' clothes could not compare to that powder blue long-sleeve T.

Your relationship with God can fit you just right too. Your parents, friends, and people at the Church can all help guide you into a loving relationship with God. But you are the one that needs to build that loving personal friendship with God. You are the one that can make your walk with God something special that will be your very own.

Don't wait; begin now thinking of ways you can draw near to God.

Memorize:

Come near to God and he will come near to you.
James 4:8a

What are some of your favorite things? Why do you like them so much?

What are some things you can do to begin making your relationship with God your very own?

Neck Stepper
by Rob Link

You my friend are a neck stepper.

Or at least are called to be one.

Feeling encouraged yet? Or just confused?

In the book of Joshua chapter 10 we see the Israelites conquering five kings who were stronger, better-equipped and thoroughly set against the move of God. Yet with God's, help victory was fast and sure.

After the enemy is defeated Joshua brings out the five enemy rulers, puts them on the ground and has the people come one at a time and put a foot on each of the five kings' necks. (See verse 24.)

What the heck is that about?

I'll tell you what it is about.

Stepping on the necks of the enemy's rulers is a powerful symbol of defeat for them and victory for you. This neck stepping is a declaration saying, "Because of the work of God we are walking in victory, freedom, and authority over the enemy of God's people."

You are called to be a neck stepper!

That is to say you are called to walk in victory, freedom and authority over that which has been set against you.

Joshua's neck stepping escapade is a poignant reminder that we are (in the words of the Apostle Paul in Romans 8) more than conquerors.

It is time for you to rise up and throw off timidity. It is time that the things that have been defeating you get put in their place – under your foot.

You my friend are a neck stepper. Start living like it.

In what areas of your life are you timid?

What would it look like for you to be a neck stepper?

Be Holy

by Ben Engbers

Therefore, with minds that are alert and fully sober, set your hope on the grace to be brought to you when Jesus Christ is revealed at his coming. As obedient children, do not conform to the evil desires you had when you lived in ignorance. But just as he who called you is holy, so be holy in all you do; for it is written: "Be holy, because I am holy."
1 Peter 1:13-16

Do you ever find yourself frustrated with how you handled a situation?

That is kind of a dumb question, because we obviously all do sometimes.

But I am talking about that thing that trips you up repeatedly. The thing that you know is wrong and yet still find yourself struggling with over and over.

These are the things that drive me crazy.

Just remember, God doesn't expect us to handle these

situations on our own.

You need to be prepared for situations before they happen, know how you want to respond, and ask God to give you strength. We often get caught up in believing the lie that our actions only impact us. This isn't true, you need to be Jesus to your friends, classmates and neighbors. Good news – Jesus wants to do the heavy lifting. He just needs you to be a good listener and a willing participant.

What steps can you take to be prepared?

Are you letting God use you?

God's Love
by Rod Tucker

For I am convinced that neither death nor live, neither angels nor demons, neither the present nor the future, nor any powers, neither height nor depth, nor anything else in all creation, will be able to separate us from the love of God that is in Christ Jesus our Lord.
Romans 8:38-39

One of the biggest pieces of who God is for us can be summed up in one word: Love. God truly does love us more than we could ever imagine. He loves us even more than we could ever love anyone. God's love for us is amazingly huge.

In Romans 8, The Apostle Paul explains to us that God's love, through Jesus is so large that not even some of the greatest powers in the universe can separate us from how much he loves us.

If we were to die tomorrow, we would still be in God's love.

If all of the angels and demons in all of heaven and hell

turned on us, we would still be in God's love.

If we did something evil and horrible now, and even if we did that same thing in the future, we would still be in God's love. In fact, nothing in all of creation (and God created everything) can separate us from the love of God.

This is all because of who Jesus is and what he did for us on the cross.

Do you know God loves you?

What do you think about God loving us this much?

BBB

by Rob Link

A while back I wrote this letter to my church;

Hello River,

Let me remind you about what I talked about on Sunday or if you weren't there inform you. I used the teaching time to remind all of us of what our vision statement is here at the River. Most organizations have a statement that helps keep them on target. A vision statement answers the questions "Who are we?" and "What do we see this place becoming?"

I taught from the book of Jonah – a man called to go and preach to the people of Nineveh. They were evil, cruel, and vicious, and Jonah wanted nothing to do with them. Yet God is persuasive, and Jonah ended up in Nineveh. He preached a short sermon, and the entire city turned to God. Amazing. These evil people were exactly the ones God wanted to extend his grace upon. That is crazy grace.

It's this crazy grace that is the foundation of our vision

statement. We see the River as a place for people to **Belong** that they might eventually **Believe** in Jesus and eventually **Become** the person God has made them to be. In many places a person's acceptance is contingent upon right behavior. When this is true many are excluded from hearing the message of this crazy grace. Since we want all to hear about this wonderful crazy grace we want people to have a place to belong so that they can hear and believe.

How have you experienced this crazy grace?

How can you help your church fulfill the vision of Belong, Believe, Become?

Play Like A Champion Today
by Todd Kingma

Whether you like, dislike, or even follow Notre Dame football, I can tell you that Notre Dame has one of the best motivational lines of all time: "Play Like A Champion Today."

Go ahead and say it again – "Play Like A Champion Today."

That's great stuff.

It's catchy.

It makes you think.

It makes you believe.

And when you believe you are a champion, you will actually play like one. Like I said, this is great stuff.

The cool thing is that the challenge to "Play Like A Champion Today" is not limited to football.

If you think about it, the statement relates to everything we do in life. Even to how we live out our faith.

And yet, too often most of us are willing to live with a timid, unseen faith. We are content not to sin too much. We are timid when it comes to acting out our faith. We hide our faith because of a fear of failure and rejection. Or, because of the negative comments from other Christians, we just quit trying.

Does that describe you? It does for most of us. And why? Because we really don't trust God and his promise that he has won the victory over sin, that we are truly forgiven, and that all we have to do is live out that victory. And so we don't live out our faith like the "champions" listed in Hebrews 11.

A well-known Christian author, Max Lucado, touched on this issue in his book "The Applause from Heaven." Here is a summary of what he wrote. Imagine that you are in an ice skating competition. You are in first place with one round to go. If you do well, you will win the trophy. You are nervous, anxious and scared. Just before you hit the ice, you learn that you won! Based on the score, no matter what you do, the second place person cannot catch you. You are too far ahead. With that news, how will you skate? Timidly? Cautiously? Afraid? Of course not. You will go out with courage and confidence. You will not be afraid to make mistakes. You will skate like a champion because that is what you are!

So think about it. You are a child of God. He has already won the victory over sin for you. You can claim that victory and be confident. Nothing can ever take you out of God's hand, and no one will ever take away your salvation.

Don't believe me? I suggest that you read a few of these texts each day for the next 21 days: Ephesians 3:12; 1 Timothy 3:13; Hebrews 4:16; 1 John 4:17; 1 Corinthians 15:27; John 5:24; Romans 8:31, 37.

They are great for giving you some spiritual boldness and confidence.

Bottom line, the pressure is off. Jesus has won the victory. So play – and live – like a champion today!

Be honest – are you afraid at times to admit your faith or act on it? If so, why?

Have you fallen for another trap by believing that if you follow Jesus you will never "fumble", get hurt, or miss a play here and there? Don't believe that lie either.

Are you playing your Christian life not to lose or are you playing like a winner?

Do you think that you need to win the victory and beat Satan? If so, remember that the Bible does not ask us to defeat Satan or win the victory. Jesus has already done that. Our task is simply to enforce the victory! Think what that looks like for you this week.

Fighting Through the Crowd
by Dan Smith

Have you ever been in the middle of a massive crowd of people? Thousands, tens of thousands, even hundreds of thousands of people crowded together to hear the colorful melodies of your favorite band, or to catch a glimpse of the game-winning field goal of your favorite football team, or even to march side by side with many others in hope of bringing awareness or raising funds to end one of the world's worst afflictions.

We find ourselves in the middle of the crowd often.

These "crowds" remind me of a story found in the scriptures. Jesus is walking through a crowd of people, a crowd that was pressing and stressing to get closer to Jesus. Word had spread that Jesus could perform any miracle and could heal any illness. Everyone, their mother, their uncle, their best friend, and their best friend's friends were flocking to Jesus to see or to receive a miracle. A woman, who had a hemorrhage for twelve years and had not found healing from anyone or anything, desperately went after Jesus, fighting through the crowd, hoping that if she could just touch even a corner of his clothing, he could heal her.

She believed so strongly that this was the man that could end her pain. If only she could just make it close enough to him that she could simply touch the hem of his garment. After years of failed attempts at being healed, she knew that on that day, by touching the garment of Jesus, she would be healed.

What's your hesitation? No, really? What's stopping you from fighting through the crowd to get to Jesus? You may be asking yourself, where is the crowd? Is there even a crowd going after Jesus like in this story? I promise you, there is. I can also promise you that you may be fighting through the crowd of people who are just hoping to witness a miracle and not actually receive one. Which are you? I'd bet cash money that you are surrounded by people who are looking to see or receive a miracle. Most are looking for the miracle in other things, but it can only be found in Jesus. That was true then, it is true now, and it will always be true.

Are you a part of the crowd? Or are you desperately fighting to get to Jesus even if to just touch the corner of his coat?

To find out what happened to the woman and how Jesus responds, read Luke 8:40-48. Thoughts?

Kings of Creation
by Rod Tucker

Then God said, "Let us make man in our image, in our likeness, and let them rule over the fish of the sea and the birds of the air, over the livestock, over all the earth, and over all the creatures that move along the ground." Genesis 1:26

When God created the world, he made us rulers. If he is the Almighty King, then we are kings below him who also rule over this creation with him. This is a huge responsibility.

Later in Genesis, when the devil tempted Adam and Eve to sin, he tried to steal some of their authority to rule over everything in Creation. Simply, the devil tried to make it so that sin ruled over Adam and Eve. However, because of Jesus dying on the cross and rising from the dead, the devil was not successful in this.

Nothing can rule over us.

God has made us kings.

So when we think about sin, whether it be pornography, anger, jealousy, un-forgiveness, or any other kind, we must know that none of these things were created to rule over us. We are the ones with authority. We are the kings. We rule over all of creation.

Because of this, we can always choose to turn to Christ for strength, help, intimacy, and forgiveness.

What do you think God meant when he told Adam to rule?

What does it mean for you to rule?

Love

by Brian Fraaza

At our house, we have a question that we ask around the dinner table. "What did you do today to make someone feel special?"

We began to do this a while back because it was a simple way to begin teaching the principle of love. God wants us to love people.

Love makes people feel special. So teaching my four-year-old to be aware of opportunities to make someone feel special is teaching her to be on the look-out for chances to love people.

Jesus was amazing at making people feel special when he came to earth. Everyone that spent time around him felt important. That's because Jesus knew that loving people was an important part of what he was here to do. He spent time with people, building lots of relationships with people, just because he knew it would make them feel special.

If you are a disciple of Jesus, you have a responsibility to love people too.

What did you do today to make someone feel special?

How about tomorrow?

Fasting. Give it a try.
by Rob Link

Hungry?

I am.

As I write this devo I'm in the midst of a little fasting season.

Fasting is a difficult thing. I wonder why they call it fasting when it seems to go so slow.

Here's what I'd like to ask you to do: fast for two days. Two days no food. Drink a ton of juice and water. No food. Two days. Try it and see what happens.

As you contemplate fasting I have two thoughts to share:

First, Jesus said to hunger and thirst for righteousness. Fasting gives us a little better perspective on what it means to hunger and thirst (see the end of Matthew 6). When fasting, take your grumbly tummy as a reminder to pray and read your word. Replace those natural cravings for food (or TV, the internet, or whatever) with time with

God. Turn on the praise music and belt it out. Listen to the Bible while you drive. Make a list of prayers you'd like to see answered – and pray the list. Use this time of hunger to increase your hunger for righteousness.

And second, when fasting, don't quit.

> *Let perseverance finish its work so that you may be mature and complete, not lacking anything.*
> *James 1:4*

Hang in there. You can do this.

As you plan this fast, maybe you need to call a brother or sister and invite them to join you. Maybe not. Either way, give fasting a chance to work its wonder in your life.

Italian Stallion

by Jason Luke

Any Rocky fans out there?

You know the story of the Italian club fighter from Philadelphia who by some odd chance got a shot at the Heavyweight Title.

Although Rocky is a fictional story, we all have this same opportunity: stay a chump or rise to the occasion. Life will throw punches regardless. The choice to engage is ours. What will you do?

For me and most of us, the attack came early, really before I was even born. My mom had many wounds from an alcoholic father that left her broken and needy. One was having me as her son when she was a very unstable teenager. By the age of nine, I had four different last names, none of which were from my biological father. I still haven't met him to this day. This lack of identity led me to making many bad choices, like being expelled from a high school and additions to drugs, alcohol, and sex. Basically, I hurt or took advantage of anyone around me for years. I was on the canvas looking up at the ref counting me out — one, two, three...

Obviously, I didn't believe that I could handle life's hard hits.

Sin ain't no joke!

It will whip your butt! Unless you ask for your eyes to get sliced opened, you may be blinded to the damage you're taking.

And then, something in me wanted more. I didn't jump straight up; I reached for the ropes to pull myself up and eventually stumbled to my feet, haggard and bloody.

So what was it in me that wanted up off my back?

John Eldredge writes in his book, *Wild at Heart*, that I was searching for the answer to the question that every man struggles with since birth, "Do I have what it takes?"

Am I the type of macho guy who poses and pretends I can handle life challenges alone? Or the passive man who runs and hides from life's difficult moments?

I was both a passive man and a poser, which meant I got pummeled.

Finally, after taking a beating for years, I began to feel it was time to fight back.

No doubt, I needed Jesus. Ultimately he was with me through the junk despite the body blows. Even though I didn't recognize his voice at first, it was his leading that said, "Get up kid. You're better than this." Like Rocky's gritty coach Mick, Jesus' belief in me started to penetrate my heart.

That's the point where "The Eye of the Tiger" kicked in and I began to chase and catch chickens.

Do you know what I'm talking about?

Be prepared because our enemy is fierce, he gets stronger, angrier much like Clubber or Ivan.

Now it's up to you. Do you have what it takes?

Dig deep. The battles get intense.

If you were the ringside ESPN sports commentator, how would you describe the fight you're in?

Do you see yourself as a champion? Why or why not?

What areas do you need more training in? What is our coach saying to you?

175lb Lap Dog
by Rob Link

I was watching the Orlando Magic the other night while sitting in my La-Z-Boy. My night was peaceful and relaxing.

That changed in the blink of an eye.

Out of nowhere Barkly jumped up on my lap. His agile antics effectively killed my comfort and interrupted the game.

In case you haven't picked up on it, Barkly is huge. He weighs 175pounds. Neither my lap nor the La-Z-Boy were expecting the added burden of that hairy beast. In addition to his girth, he brought a fair amount of slobber with him, which ended up grossly smeared on my sweatshirt.

So there I was with a huge drool machine sitting on my lap interrupting my well-planned evening.

And I loved it. A lot.

In fact this is one of the reasons I love Newfies. As a breed they are known for their affectionate nature. It is as if they can't help but be loving and affectionate.

Barkly is happiest when he is closest to me.

And sometimes that means my plans get interrupted. And as I've said I love it.

Seems to me that God is a lot like that. Not the slobbering dog part, but the loves affection part – even when it is seemingly ill-timed and messy.

The Bible makes it clear that the Lord loves the praise of his people. Often in the scriptures we see the Lord's presence visiting the people when they praise (go to *biblos.com* and do some searching of your own). He loves it when we go all Newfy on him. That is to say, God really appreciates when we praise him, tell him we love him, and express our thanks to him.

How about we let our life go to the dogs – Newfoundlands to be exact. Let's learn from Barkly and hop on the lap of our Abba and lavish some affection on him.

What is your favorite worship CD? Go listen to it right now.

Wisdom and Love
by Rod Tucker

Do not arouse or awaken love until it so desires.
Song of Songs 2:7b

When the Bible talks about not awakening love until it so desires, it is speaking of something incredibly deep: our hearts.

The purpose of a person's heart are deep waters,
but one who has insight draws them out.
Proverbs 20:5

The heart is deceitful above all things and beyond cure.
Who can understand it?
Jeremiah 17:9

Sometimes our heart and our mind can be in conflict. We may feel like we want something in a relationship even though we know it is not in our best interest to go there. This is when we must become men of understanding. But the good news is that we do not have to do this on our own. God knows that our hearts can be deeper than we know and so he offers us wisdom, if we only ask.

If any of you lacks wisdom, you should ask God, who give generously to all without finding fault, and it will be given to you.
James 1:5

Having wisdom will help us to not awaken love until it is in God's timing for our lives.

What do you see at school in regard to relationships between boys and girls?

What advice would you give to one of your friends about dating?

What are your thoughts on you dating?

Courage
by Wil Crooks

At 12 years old, heights terrified me (still do). I was at the local swimming pool, and they had a high dive. All of my friends were jumping off the 15' diving board, screaming and laughing as they plummeted into the water. They were having so much fun. It couldn't be that bad, I thought, so up the ladder I climbed. Step by step my legs and arms began to shake – fear was setting in. I got to the top and walked the plank. I peered over the end of the diving board and froze. Everyone started shouting, "Hurry up and jump, Wil, hurry up." I was frozen. Kids were on every step of the ladder waiting for me to jump so they could go next. Still frozen, I turned around and walked back to the ladder and told everyone to get off because I was coming down. I came down defeated.

Everyone has things they are afraid of. But some fears must be overcome as you become God's warrior. One of the scariest fears to overcome is to stand up for what is right. Have you ever watched a kid bully another kid and then other people jump in? You know it's not right – but what do you do? We must be strong enough to come alongside the hurting and care for them. Have your friends ever wanted you to do something you knew wasn't right? Have you ever wanted to talk to your friends about God, but just felt scared to do it? It's so difficult sometimes to stand up for what is right. It's scary because you may be rejected by your friends or get talked about.

It's okay to be afraid…but we can't let fear stand in the way of standing up for Truth. When you stand up for what is right, it is God's strength that begins to work through you. And that's a really awesome power!

Memorize:
Be strong and very courageous.
Joshua 1:7a

What are you scared of and what do you do when you encounter it?

Have you ever stood up for what is right when other people were doing something wrong?

Identity Crisis
by Rob Link

I read a crazy stat the other day. Americans spend over $480 billion (yes I said billion!) each year on weight loss.

That's each year! Holy Cow!

Gym memberships that go unused.

Treadmills for the home that become laundry racks.

Diet programs that never work.

$480 billion.

Each year.

Oh my.

This is really sad. So many people not happy with who they are and/or what they look like. So many people enslaved to either food or body image or worse – both.

To be sure America is one of the most obese nations in the

world. But this $480 billion nonsense is not an obesity issue.

It's a crisis of identity.

Here's what I mean. We (and I mean "we" as I've been a part of the $480 billion madness) don't really know who we are. At the core, deep down, in our inner most being we do not know who we are. If we did, there would be freedom from this craziness.

So let me remind us who we are.

We are children of the king, fearfully and wonderfully made. Adopted into eternal nobility. A royal nation. A holy priesthood. Crafted while still in the womb. Made specifically by the hand of God – just as we are. Loved. Chosen. Called. Appointed. Perfectly formed.

That's who we are. Go back and read that last paragraph, but do it with your heart and not just your head.

Now read it again, but this time ask the Holy Spirit to help the truth sink in. You'll need help with this because the world we live in has told you and me that we aren't thin enough/are too thin/not tall enough/are too tall/too bald/too hairy… Since we were little we've been bombarded with lies saying we are not enough, we aren't quite right, we aren't ideal.

Hogwash. Reread that paragraph and ask the Spirit to pierce your soul with this awesome truth.

There is freedom in truth. Jesus said it would set us free. If we really knew these truths we wouldn't run to food for comfort or pleasure. We wouldn't run to diets and gyms in desperation. We wouldn't buy useless treadmills.

We would be free.

And in our freedom we would walk in balance letting neither food nor body image rule us. We wouldn't look in the mirror and panic. We wouldn't see that billboard of that muscular dude or skinny chick and feel horrible about ourselves. We wouldn't walk in shame because of our skinniness/fatness/tallness/shortness/etc.

We would be free. And in our freedom we would actually like ourselves.

Go back and reread this devo again.

Knucklehead
by Rob Link

Read some of Jacob's story (In Gen. 25:29-34 and 27:1-37 you can find two stories to give you a glimpse of the man). Here is what I've noticed about him. He cheated his brother out of his birthright. He cheated that same brother out of the father's blessing. He tricked his father in law, Laban, by breeding the sheep in such a way that increased his flock and shrunk Laban's. My goodness even at birth he came out grasping his brothers heal and thus was given the name Jacob meaning "usurper." Yikes. What a scoundrel.

And yet this is the knucklehead that God chose to fulfill his promise to Abraham through. I would think that God would choose someone a bit more stable.

Yet Jacob's shortcomings are not the point. Rather God's grace, mercy, and crazy love are. God extends his blessing solely out of his grace and mercy and not based on human merit. God chooses to bless morons like Jacob. God blesses the most unlikely of people. God's kingdom is advanced by fail-able goofballs. God's love and blessing are unexplainable.

Here's something cool – we too are knucklehead, moronic, goofballs just like Jacob. Even better – all those cool things about God apply to us too. Cool.

What is your gut reaction to Jacob?

What are some of your knucklehead moments?

Thank God he uses goofballs like you.

What Can I Gain?
by Dan Smith

But whatever things were gain to me, those things I have counted as loss for the sake of Christ. More than that, I count all things to be loss in view of the surpassing value of knowing Christ Jesus my Lord, for whom I have suffered the loss of all things, and count them but rubbish so that I may gain Christ. Philippians 3:7-8

In our world today, we think a lot about what we can gain. In almost every situation we find ourselves in, we think about ME first. We frequently ask, "What's in it for me?" Former NFL receiver Terrell Owens says it this way, "I love me some me."

Chances are if you play on any athletic team, you've questioned your coach on how much playing time you receive. Your favorite NBA player wants to know how much money he'll make before signing the shoe deal.

On the flip side, Jesus asks us to consider all things as loss, yes, even your playing time or the shoe deal. In Philippians 3:8 (check it out), Paul considers having and knowing Christ as being far greater than having or knowing anything else. One of my favorite authors A.W. Tozer explains it this way:

> When the Lord divided Canaan among the tribes of Israel, Levi received no share of the land. God said to him simply, "I am thy part and thine inheritance," and by those words made him richer than all his brethren, richer than all kings who have ever lived in the world. And there is a spiritual principle here, a principle still valid for every priest of the Most High God.
>
> The man who has God for his treasure has all things in One. Many ordinary treasures may be denied him, or if he is allowed to have them, the enjoyment of them will be so tempered that they will never be necessary to his happiness. Or if he must see them go, one after one, he will scarcely feel a sense of loss, for having the Source of all things he has in One all satisfaction, all pleasure, all delight. Whatever he may lose he has actually lost nothing, for he now has it all in One, and he has it purely, legitimately and forever.

Do you view a relationship with Christ as having all that you need?

Are you ready to leave things behind, so that you will gain Christ? What do you need to leave behind?

Loneliness Stinks
by Rob Link

As iron sharpens iron, so one man sharpens another. Proverbs 27:17

Throughout the scriptures it is clear that we have been made for deep, rich, raw, authentic, honest, joyful community. Yet for a multitude of reasons this reality is hard to come by. More than one of you has emailed me saying it is a nice yet unattainable theory. It is so hard to find such friendships.

So what do we do? Do we simply shake our heads in resignation and say, "It will work for someone else but not me"? In many ways this would be easier. We could grieve the loss and then move on.

Or could we?

Our hearts were made for this deep connection. Even if in our heads we can set it aside our innards will yearn for it until we find it or until we pass into glory. So I recommend not "moving on" and categorizing this notion of community and rich friendship as unattainable.

I'm thinking of Hannah from the Old Testament. She wanted a child so bad yet had been barren for so long. Amidst the sorrow and longing she repeatedly cried out to the Lord – so much so that a priest thought she was drunk. Eventually (much longer than she would have liked) she conceived and gave birth to Samuel. Out of her deepest longing and pain came the most beautiful thing in her life.

My word to all of you longing for deep friendship is twofold. First, I am sorry. It stinks to be lonely and it stinks worse to be lonely over a long period of time. Second, go the way of Hannah. Pray. Cry out. Solicit the prayers of others. Pray some more. Cry out again. And hope. Hope that the Lord truly will give you the desires of your heart. Hope that the Lord really does have a plan for you – a plan not to harm you but to give you a hope and a future. My prayer is that you lonely folks would find deep connection.

List a few names of folks you could invite to join you in a community group. Contact them today.

If you can't think of anyone, visit the "Starting Point" booth at church this Sunday.

Love Worth Finding
by Thomas Wrench

No, in all these things we are more than conquerors through him who loved us. For I am convinced that neither death nor life, neither angels nor demons, neither the present nor the future, nor any powers, neither height nor depth, nor anything else in all creation, will be able to separate us from the love of God that is in Christ Jesus our Lord.
Romans 8:37-39

There is a battle for our hearts.

We live in a broken world, a world where it seems we have no control over the things that happen.

We find ourselves at school, or with our friends, we see things in the news, we hear about injustice around the world and we feel helpless.

There's nothing we can do.

We have no control.

Control is a funny word. Control means that we are separating ourselves from the will of God. Separating ourselves from who we are destined to be.

Battle lost.

We might decide that we can do something. We can help out. We can tell people, we can raise money, we can…We can…But will these efforts fall short? Could we lose sight of whom we are fighting for? Fearful for what might come next?

Battle lost.

Take heart.

Christ redeems.

In him, we find our strength to battle on. There is nothing on this earth that can take that away. In the brokenness, in the sorrow – in the light. Christ's love for us is there.

If we seek the Lord prior to battle, we will know what to do. We will know where to be. That love for us is ever-present. That love is the answer to the questions we cannot answer.

God's love is fighting for us. He is ready to show you the way. He has your name on a stone, destined to fulfill his will for you. Seek him, and it will be revealed to you.

Imagine fighting for the Lord, as hard as he is fighting for you. It's said, "…not even the powers of Hell can separate us from God's love."

He's here. He is all in.

He's waiting for you to fight for him.

What would it look like for you to fight for him?

Daddy

by Rob Link

Abba. Aramaic for father, dad, or even daddy. Abba.

To Jesus' original audience addressing God this way was unheard of – even obscene in its familiarity. After all God was powerful and distant. Mighty and aloof. To be feared and kept at arms length. Certainly not Abba. Certainly not close and tender. Surely not intimate and affectionate.

Maybe Jesus made a mistake in addressing God as Abba.

Or maybe not.

Maybe Jesus knew exactly what he was doing. Maybe he chose to reveal the Father as Father! Maybe he knew that people had mistakenly removed the intimate and kind nature of God. And maybe he wanted to do something about it. Abba. One commentator says that the word Abba is the word uttered by a small child, barely able to talk, as he sits securely and safely on his daddy's lap and affectionately plays with his Abba's beard. That's great imagery. And it is the exact imagery that Jesus conjured when he used the word Abba.

We are his children and he is Abba. Let me say that again – we are his children and he is our Abba. He loves us more than we can imagine. Abba. Father. Dad. Daddy. God.

Read Matt. 6:9.

Ask Abba to show you his love today.

Dodge Ram
by Rob Link

A while back my older brother bequeathed us a 13-year-old truck. It was given as a beater truck for the kids to learn to drive in. In reality, the "beater" is a pretty sweet truck. In spite of being 13 years old it is in remarkable shape. The truth is my brother could have sold it for a good bit or traded it in when he bought a new vehicle. The fact that he chose to give it to us is pretty sweet. Truly a remarkable gift that was rather touching for me and my family.

Why is it that the gift of a truck evokes some strong feeling (rightly so), but the gift of the cross can fall into the oh-yeah-I've-heard-that-before category?

The immediacy and tangible nature of the truck makes it easy to deeply feel the gratitude. The intangible, can't-see-it nature of the cross makes it much more difficult to feel gratitude deeply. That's unfortunate as the gift of life that Jesus gave is much cooler than the gift of a truck.

I'm wondering if, at times, you too struggle with the intangible nature of Jesus.

What might you and your family do to combat the "intangible" nature of Jesus so that gratitude might rise?

Take some time and write out some of the blessings you have received from Abba.

Flexibility is a tough thing.
by Rob Link

Have you ever had your mind set on one thing only to find that one thing is at odds with the thoughts of others?

Kinda stinks.

When such times arise we have a few options.

We can say, "Screw it, it's my way or the highway." We can mope and be sad, playing the martyr. We can get angry and throw a fit.

Or we can be flexible.

The Apostle Paul says to consider others as better than yourselves. (See Philippians 2:3.)

This isn't easy.

But it is the way of Christ.

Even though it is tough, I recommend the way of flexibility.

In what areas is it tough for you to be flexible?

Who is someone you know who is flexible?

Listening to God
by Rod Tucker

"But the Advocate, the Holy Spirit whom the Father will send in my name, will teach you all things and will remind you of everything I have said to you."
John 14:26

God has sent us his Holy Spirit to teach us.

Another way of saying this is that God speaks to us through his Holy Spirit.

Sometimes when I sit alone and listen for God to speak to me I take a pad of paper and a pen. I write down everything that I think God is saying to me and then I go and check it out in the Bible and with a close friend or parent. There are many things that God wants us to hear.

Sometimes we can even hear from God how we are supposed to pray for someone we have not spoken to that day. Or God might even tell us to tell someone else something from him.

God desires to use us radically for his glory and his

Kingdom because he wants people everywhere to know him. For that we need to take the time and listen to him and hear what he has to say.

Take a moment to sit down and "listen" for God to tell you something. Write what he says below or on a separate piece of paper.

Dog Gone Dagon!
by Rob Link

There is a story in the book of 1 Samuel where the Philistines capture the Ark of the Covenant and place it alongside the idol of their God Dagon. In the Old Testament the Ark was the center of God's presence on earth. The Philistines thought that they had hit pay day when they captured the Ark and could add it to their day-to-day list of things they worshipped.

God thought differently.

After the first night the Philistines found the idol of Dagon knocked over, lying face down in front of the Ark. They propped it back up and went about their business.

The next morning not only did they find it face down again, this time its arms had broken off. It was at this point the Philistines realized that God's presence wasn't to be trifled with and sent the Ark back into Israelite territory.

A few lessons for us:
- We, like the Philistines, think that we can add God to a list of good things.

- God will not allow Himself to simply be relegated to one of many. He will (in his time) knock down the things we have set up that keep us from having him be Lord of all.
- We, like the Philistines, are slow learners. After things that need to be knocked down are knocked down, we stubbornly prop them up again.
- God will be faithful to remind us that he is Lord and nothing else. The more we resist and keep propping things up, the more drastic the reminder (i.e. the idols arms were broken off the second time).
- It is worth reflecting on the troubles we are bumping up against. It could be (note I said could be) that God is trying to remind us that he is Lord and will not compete against the other things of life.
- It seems it would be easier to examine ourselves and remove the things that we have set up alongside God ourselves so we don't have to run into the correction of the Lord.

Light
by Wil Crooks

My favorite game as a kid was hide-n-go-seek IN THE DARK. Oh what fun that was. I always got so excited finding my hiding spot and then waiting – I got so excited that I had to go pee the minute I found my spot. It never failed – the agony and excitement of it all was so much fun.

The goal was not to be found and by staying in the dark it was harder for anyone to find me. The darker it was and the quieter I was, the harder it was to find me.

Sometimes when we do things that are wrong we would rather hide them versus telling someone. Other times we are growing up and get scared to ask questions: questions about girls, our bodies changing, or struggles we are having in school. It's just easier to keep things hidden so that we can deal with it alone, in the dark.

But the better way to live is in the light. Hiding things or being afraid to ask questions is living in the dark and the dark can be very dangerous. The enemy loves to lie to you when you live in the dark. However, when you live in the light – when you tell people when you were wrong and you have the courage to ask hard questions – you are able to live joyful, safe, and free. Light drives away darkness. Living a life in the light is a strong and Godly way to live.

Memorize:
> *Live as children of light...*
> *Ephesians 5:8b*

And Yet...

by Rob Link

The Bible says about itself, "All scripture is God-breathed and is useful for teaching, rebuking, correcting, and training" (2 Timothy 3:16).

And sometimes I say about the Bible, "It seems impersonal and boring."

You ever felt that way? Have you ever heard a message on the power of the Bible, got pumped to read it, and then found yourself let down?

I have. On more occasions than I'd like.

And yet...

And yet there are times that the word jumps off the page as if God had me and just me in mind when the words were written.

And yet there are times when the word is so poignant and pertinent that I have to stop, reread, and take a moment to soak it in.

And yet there are times that I get caught up in the narrative that I feel like I'm reading a best seller (which in fact I am – The Bible is the best selling book of all time).

These awesome Biblical watershed moments would never have come had I quit reading it when I was bored. The perseverance has paid off on many occasions even though I wanted to throw in the towel on reading the Bible many times.

So here's the deal. I'd like for you to take a month long challenge and read the Bible every day. Have a journal with you so you can record the things that jump out at you.

I recommend you read Judges, or 1 & 2 Samuel. Enjoy the stories. Ask God to speak to you through the stories. Ask yourself if you can relate with any of the characters. Read. Fight through the boredom. And have your own "and yet" moment.

What Jesus Felt
by Brian Bensinger

I think a lot of times Jesus seems like this far off, unapproachable guy. He's God, way up in Heaven – how can he know what's going on with me, or what I'm feeling? We often focus on him being just God, forgetting that he was once a human, just like us. In fact, Jesus wanted to experience what we do, so he would have something in common with us. It's easy to say, "Well that was easy for Jesus, he's God." But I don't think it was always easy for him. I know it wasn't.

Since the children have flesh and blood, he too shared in their humanity so that by his death he might break the power of him who holds the power of death – that is, the devil – and free those who all their lives were held in slavery by their fear of death. For surely it is not angels he helps, but Abraham's descendants. For this reason he had to be made like them, fully human in every way, in order that he might become a merciful and faithful high priest in service to God, and that he might make atonement for the sins of the people. Because he himself suffered when he was tempted, he is able to help those who are being tempted.
Hebrews 2:14-18.

He shared in our humanities. He had to be made like his brothers (us) in every way so that he could be a merciful and high priest for us. Every emotion you've ever felt: loneliness, sorrow, grief, worry, emptiness, betrayal, temptation, along with the emotions that bring you happiness, joy, laughter, excitement, and fulfillment, Jesus has felt. He knows exactly what you are going through. Just as Hebrews 4 says (check it out sometime), we have a high priest who is able to sympathize with our weaknesses and One who wants you to come talk to him with boldness, confidence, and hope, knowing that our Father is delighted in you and wishes to help you through life.

When Jesus was finished teaching at the end of John chapter 6 his disciples were still doubting and grumbling. Some were leaving him. How do you think this made Jesus feel? Notice he says, "You do not want to leave too, do you?" Jesus must have felt saddened. He must have felt lonely. He must have felt fully human - just like you. He still calls today. His desire is to give you bread and water so that you will never hunger or thirst again. And when times of hunger and thirst come, he is right there, knowing exactly what you are feeling, wanting nothing more than to help you.

What does it mean to have a God who knows what's it's like to be you? What does it say about Jesus who left

Heaven to be like us and share in the human experience?

Does Jesus seem easy to talk to, like a close friend, or does he seem far away, and more like a principal who is ready to scold you? Why or why not?

Do you believe what God said when he says to approach his throne with boldness and hope, knowing he is ready to give you grace and comfort? Do you pray this way?

What do you want?
by Rob Link

Admiral Perry first stated that he wanted to reach the north pole at the age of 10. Amazing. Throughout his adolescence and early adulthood many folks (in fact a majority of folks) who heard his dream discouraged him. Yet he was of a single mind and pursued the dream relentlessly. He wanted it. He made it happen.

I was reading in a devotional the following: "When I hear someone say, 'I always wanted to be a teacher,' only politeness keeps me from answering, 'No you didn't, or you'd be a teacher. There was no "always" and you didn't really "want it." You just had a little wishfulness now and then.'"

Yikes - that's pretty in your face. And right on the money. Let's be honest if we really want something, really want it, we will work for it tirelessly. Much of what we say we want is really only wishfulness or even worse lip-service.

The Psalmist says, "As the deer pants for streams of water, so my soul pants for you, my God" (Psalm 42:1). Really?

Really? I don't know about you. I would like this to be true for me. But it often isn't.

Do I really want to be close to God? Do you? Do I really desire to be intimate with him at all cost? Do you? If so we would do what it takes. Maybe the first step is to pray that our wishfulness meets reality. I'd love to go the way of Admiral Bird in my pursuit of the Lord. Wouldn't you?

Stop and pray. Ask God to change your wishfulness into reality. If you'd like, write your prayer here.

Living Honestly
by Rod Tucker

But if we walk in the light, as he is in the light, we have fellowship with one another, and the blood of Jesus, his Son, purifies us from all sin.
1 John 1:7

God desires that we live in the light with each other.

This means living honestly.

If we claim to be without sin, we deceive ourselves and the truth is not in us.
1 John 1:8

If I am not living an honest lifestyle, then there is great possibility that I am looking like I am not sinning when there really is sin in my life.

However, if I can find people in my life with whom I can be honest when I sin, then I can have fellowship and know that Jesus' blood has covered all of my guilt.

If you do not have someone in your life that you can live

in honesty with, someone who can help you grow in your life with Christ, it is important for you to pray about this, talk to your parent(s) or someone close to you, and find a trustworthy person who can come alongside you and help.

There are many people around where you live who would love to be part of your life.

Who can you "live honestly with?"

What can you share with them – what have you been hiding?

91%
by Rob Link

Not so long ago, I was in Tulare, California just 45 minutes south of Fresno at a church planting conference. The gathering was for pastors who have either already started a new church or will be shortly. While there I heard a staggering statistic. Gallup did a study on 300 new churches that failed. 91% of the churches failed for the same reason. What do you think it was?

Incompetent pastor? Nope.

Poor worship music? Nope.

Stinky youth ministries? Nope.

Uncoordinated childcare? Nope.

The reason 91% of the churches failed had absolutely nothing to do with a lack of competency.

So what was it?

The cause for so many failed churches was character/

moral failure of the leadership. Yikes. Affairs. Embezzlement. Power lust. Ego mania. Sexual impropriety. Financial greediness. These are the things that kill the church. Character failure is incredibly costly to the advancement of the Kingdom of God.

Well, guess what, people. Character failure is not just something that affects church leadership detrimentally. It affects all of Christ's followers negatively. Just because you are not starting a new church does not mean you can ignore holiness and skate by without consequence. You let your character slip and it will come back to bite you in the butt.

I told these pastors the same thing I am telling you. The best way to prevent moral/character failure in your life is to walk closely with Jesus. Make the time daily to read your Bible (maybe start with a Bible through the year plan), pray (I suggest writing your prayers – lends focus) and listen to what the Lord might say to you (again a journal is helpful for you to record what you hear). Get with the Lord regularly and just watch what happens!

What do you think about the reason 91% of churches fail?

What safeguards can you put in place to guard your heart?

Set Free
by Dan Smith

Jesus is and has always been about catapulting people from death to life – even before Jesus, himself, went from death to life. In John 8, we find one of the best stories of grace, mercy, and love found in the Bible. Check this out:

But Jesus went to the Mount of Olives. At dawn he appeared again in the temple courts, where all the people gathered around him, and he sat down to teach them. The teachers of the law and the Pharisees brought in a woman caught in adultery. They made her stand before the group and said to Jesus, "Teacher, this woman was caught in the act of adultery. In the Law Moses commanded us to stone such women. Now what do you say?" They were using this question as a trap, in order to have a basis for accusing him.

But Jesus bent down and started to write on the ground with his finger. When they kept on questioning him, he straightened up and said to them, "If any one of you is without sin, let him be the first to throw a stone at her." Again he stooped down and wrote on the ground. At this, those who heard began to go away one at a time, the older ones first, until only Jesus was left, with the woman still standing there. Jesus straightened up and asked her, "Woman, where are they? Has no one condemned you?"

"No one, sir," she said.

"Then neither do I condemn you," Jesus declared. "Go now and leave your life of sin."
John 8:1-11

Jesus was thrown into controversy and put on the spot. What the Pharisees meant as a trap, Jesus used to set someone free. Set free from death and free to fully live.

How do you respond in times when the world seems to be against you? Does panic set in?

Are you often stressed and possibly frustrated? The way Jesus handled this situation is genius. I want to be there. I want to be able to receive that kind of grace and give that kind of grace. This is the kind of encounter we see Jesus in all around us, with us, and with everyone.

My prayer is that we would be the kind of people that open our lives up to receive this kind of response from Jesus and then offer the same response to others. I want a chance at redemption and a shot at new life, a different life, and a life of great value. Jesus is always looking for opportunities to move us from death to life.

Do you think any of the Pharisees in this story were moved to greater hope, faith, and purpose? I believe that at least one probably was. One person is worth it. One life is worth it for Jesus. Your life is worth it for Jesus.

Memorial Day
by Rob Link

I like Memorial Day. Picnics, burgers, watermelons, welcoming summer, parks, hot dogs – these are the things that fill the day for many of us.

You probably know that the original intent of Memorial Day was for us as a nation to take a time-out from our day-to-day activities and remember the ultimate sacrifice countless men and women have paid in service to our country.

A great idea.

When you look around the globe it is hard to not notice how privileged we are, how abundant life is, and how wonderful our freedoms happen to be.

I was talking with someone who has spent some time in Uganda. He said the doctors in Uganda make less than anyone on welfare in our country. Wow. For many reasons, this is a great country. It is right for us to remember those who died that we might walk in freedom.

Hmm. Dying that others might walk in freedom. Sounds like Jesus to me. After all, he paid the ultimate price so that we would not have to. The difference is that whereas our brave men and women died for a freedom that we can't take with us when we die, Jesus' death enables us to live in a freedom that goes with us into eternity. Whereas the gallant soldiers who died remain dead, Jesus sprang from the empty tomb. No death could hold him down. And thus we can live a life not only of freedom, but also a life of victory.

Whatever time of year it is, make today a memorial day where you remember the men and women who died so we could be free.

Take a moment to remember what the cross and empty tomb mean to you.

Wireless
by Todd Kingma

Words are interesting.

One reason – over time, many words can take on new or additional meanings.

For example, when I grew up, "text" meant a course book used at school; "cloud" meant that white, fluffy stuff in the sky; "mail" was something that a mailman delivered to our house; and "wireless" meant the very limited and old form of communication sent by telegraph.

Today, "text" is an electronic message sent from a mobile phone; the "cloud" is where electronic data is stored; "mail" now includes electronic messages that no mailman will ever see or deliver; and "wireless" refers to virtually everything associated with communication – computers, printers and phones.

And as sure as you are reading this devotional, words that are common to you today will certainly be used differently in just a few short years.

But I have found one word – or name – to be constant: Jesus.

The dictionary describes "Jesus" as the Jewish teacher whose life, death and resurrection are the basis of the Christian faith.

That's it. Nothing more; nothing less.

There is, of course, the option of choice. You can either choose to believe in Jesus or not. But that choice will not change the fact that, in the Christian faith, salvation is incredibly simple. Jesus is the one Savior. No new meaning. No additional meaning.

Just Jesus.

> *In the beginning was the Word [i.e Jesus], and the Word was with God, and the Word was God.*
> *John 1:1*
>
> *The woman said, "I know that Messiah" (called Christ) "is coming. When he comes, he will explain everything to us." Then Jesus declared, "I, the one speaking to you—I am he."*
> *John 4:25-26.*

So today and throughout this week, give this Jesus, this consistent one, some thought. Read John 14:6-7; 1 Corinthians 8:5-6; Galatians 4:4; and Philippians 2:7-8. And remember, when you hear someone say that Jesus is the same yesterday, today and in the days to come, know that they are right.

There is something cool about this consistency. Something that leads people like me to him. I urge you to check him out for yourself today and to get to know him better.

You will be glad you did.

What words can you think of that have a different meaning today than when you first heard the word earlier?

What does "Jesus" mean to you?

I read something a while back that said if people want to learn about God, they can look at Jesus. If people want to learn about Jesus, they should be able to look at his followers. Can they see Jesus in you?

Wireless 2
by Todd Kingma

When I grew up, we were all "wired."

I suppose that suggests we were all a little bit edgy, but it really means that we were always connected to something. Our phones were connected to the wall by long, curly cords; otherwise, they would not work. Our televisions were connected to antennas that were on the roof of our homes; otherwise, we would have no picture at all. For those rare souls who actually had a printer, they were connected by several cords to the computer; otherwise, no printing.

Today, well, it's all "wireless."

No cords connecting phones to the wall. Everyone has a mobile phone.

No antennas mounted on everyone's roof; rather, television comes in via satellite.

And printers, like the phones, are rarely connected to anything.

All the connections are wireless. 3G, 4G…fast, faster. No connections.

And yet, so many people today do NOT feel connected to anything, to anyone or to any faith.

As a result, we are slowly losing our connections with people, and even with our God. We really don't trust or depend on anyone or anything. While we are encouraged to be men – do it on your own, be self sufficient, etc. – we are actually living a lame, weak, connection-less life and faith.

But it does not have to be that way. The Bible is full of examples of men who were connected to God – they trusted and depended on him, and on him alone.

Here are just a few examples:

> *Joshua:*
> *"…choose for yourselves this day whom you will serve…as for me and my household, we will serve the Lord."*
> *Joshua 24:15b*
>
> *Shadrach, Meshach and Abednego:*
> *"…we do not need to defend ourselves before you…the*

God we serve is able to deliver us from [the furnace]… But even if he does not, we want you to know, Your Majesty, that we will not serve your gods or worship the image of gold you have set up."
Daniel 3:16-18

Paul:
I care very little if I am judged by you or by any human court…It is the Lord who judges me.
1 Corinthians 4:3-4

Wow!

Why were they able to do and say the things they did? Because they were connected – connected to the God they believed in.

So think about this today. While at school, at home, at work – wherever you are – stay connected to God. Trust and depend on him to make a difference in your life.

Do you feel connected to anyone or anything? If so, who or what? If not, why?

If you spent more time with God by reading and studying his word, do you think it would help you form a better connection with him? If so, what is stopping you from doing so?

How can you stay connected with your faith? List some things you can do to avoid being "disconnected."

Food

by Rob Link

I played hoops the other day.

About croaked.

You see I was in the midst of a bit of fasting and it had been a few days since I had eaten anything. So when I went to run up and down the court – the tank was empty. The feeling in my body was just bizarre. What would be a normal, no problem jaunt from one end to the other left me with my hands on my knees with my heart pounding. While playing I knew what I wanted to do – my body just wouldn't respond. If you need a reminder, take it from me: the body needs food to function properly.

The same is true for the spiritual body. Jesus said that we do not live by bread alone but by every word that comes from the mouth of God (Matthew 4:4).

The Word.

The Scriptures.

The Bible.

This is the nutrition the soul needs to function properly.

A Christ follower without any Word in him/her is like me trying to play basketball with no food in my system. You just won't function the way you were meant to function.

Too many of us go through life devoid of any of the good food for the soul.

Here is what I think you ought to do this week. Read at least one verse a day for the next 7 days. And then if you can get through the week try it again for the next week. And then if you can get through that week try it again the next week. You'll find you have more energy and fuel for your inner, spiritual man/woman.

Jon O.

by Rob Link

Ozzy isn't his real name. His real name is Jon Osbourne. I recently read his autobiography, *I Am Ozzy*.

Wow. I learned a few things about Ozzy.

First off, he swears like a sailor – make that three sailors.

Secondly, it is truly amazing he isn't dead from the abuse he put his body through for decades.

Thirdly, the book was filled with him articulating disappointment, embarrassment, and regret for the life he has lived.

What became readily apparent to me as I read about Ozzy is the fact that he is a wounded, broken man who used to be a wounded, broken little boy. His life has been spent in the pursuit of meaning, significance and acceptance. He has spent millions of dollars on drugs, alcohol, etc. in effort to escape his pain. He couldn't do it.

Now that he is sober (has been for a few years now) his life is marked with remorse and regret.

Ozzy had all the things that money, fame, and success could buy. Cars, homes, vacations, drugs, sex. Yet none of it brought him happiness.

None of it.

While reflecting back on his life Ozzy doesn't see peace and joy. He see's remorse and regret. He learned a hard lesson over the years – stuff (material goods, drugs, etc.) is not the source of fulfillment and abundant living.

I think to a lesser degree we are all like Ozzy. Seeking belonging, purpose, and significance in things that will only prove to be empty. As I read the book I was given a poignant reminder that only in Jesus is life found. Only in Jesus is there peace that passes understanding. And only in Jesus is there joy that transcends circumstance.

How are you like Ozzy?

Best Effort
by Rob Link

Rod and I have been co-coaching the 8th grade boys' basketball team at Maple Street Middle School for a few years. Each day during the season, we encourage these young men to give their best effort. When we see them slowing down due to fatigue or distraction we stop practice and take the moment to teach. We teach them that as coaches we would be doing them a disservice to allow them to continue on in practice not giving their best effort. We tell them that the only way to improve themselves is to continually give all that they have. We ask them if they are willing to give all they got so that at the end of the day they can go home and tell their family they gave all they had.

Interestingly as the weeks go by each season, we see a desire grow in these young men to push themselves to the point of exhaustion. After having run to the point of almost vomiting, they lay on the ground panting with enormous grins on their young faces. They have discovered the joy of hard work.

Part of the joy comes from the fact that they are giving

their best as a team. There is an encouragement when you go through practice (or life) giving extreme effort alongside teammates who love you and encourage you.

Here is the point for us. The cost of following Christ is high. To be sure his grace and mercy are free. Yet to be fully sold out to Jesus – which is what he wants from us – is a tough thing. What I've learned from those young men at Maple Street is that it is worth the hard work to put in the effort to grow in Christ through the disciplines of prayer, fasting, studying the word, etc.

Brothers and sisters, find your team with whom you can struggle through this practice we call life, and give your best effort to walk into the fullness of who Christ has called you to become.

Who might be on your "team?"

What does your best effort in your faith journey look like?

It Rained. A lot.
by Rob Link

A few years back, I took Jake, our then 13-year-old son, and four of his 13-year-old buddies backpacking down in the Smokey Mountains. We arrived at our spot around 7:30 Friday night. We had a three-hour hike down the mountain ahead of us. Things got interesting when the sun went down an hour in and it was pitch black with two hours to go. Things got even more interesting when, with an hour and a half to get to the campsite, the skies opened up and the rain fell in torrential sheets.

One young man kept saying, "Mr. Link we missed the turn! We missed the turn!" Another said repeatedly, "We're lost, we're lost!" A third was quietly crying. His nerves were shot.

But one young man was as peaceful and joyful as can be. While the others were nervous and scared, he was relaxed and confident without a care in the world.

What was the difference?

The difference was the fact that he was walking closest to

Jake, the son. This peaceful young man was Jake's tent partner and closest friend amongst the group. He was the one who had spent the most time at our house just hanging around. He had had Jake over to his place multiple times. Compared to the other three he knew the son very well.

And the son knew the father.

Jake knew that his dad (me) had been a backpacking guide for years. He knew that my experience as a backcountry guide were more than enough to overcome some rain and darkness. Jake trusted his dad to see things through.

He knew and trusted his father. And the peaceful, joyful young man caught the optimism directly from the son.

Do you see where this is going? The best way to have peace and joy in life – even when it's dark and rainy – is to walk closely with the son, Jesus. He knows his father's heart and will implicitly.

The best way to walk in the blessings of the Father is to know his son. So walk with Jesus, my friends.

Will you walk closely to the son (with prayer, Bible study, etc.)?

Who is the Greatest?
by Ben Engbers

Whether talking sports or music or whatever you are in to, isn't this something we love to discuss: who is the greatest? Whether it is Michael Jordan, Tiger Woods, or Shaun White, we always want to hold up those we consider great at whatever they do.

Ironically, greatness in God's eyes is looked at much differently.

> *They came to Capernaum. When he was in the house, he asked them, "What were you arguing about on the road?" But they kept quiet because on the way they had argued about who was the greatest. Sitting down, Jesus called the Twelve and said, "Anyone who wants to be first must be the very last, and the servant of all." He took a little child whom he placed among them. Taking the child in his arms, he said to them, "Whoever welcomes one of these little children in my name welcomes me; and whoever welcomes me does not welcome me but the one who sent me."*
> *Mark 9:33-37*

Not exactly the way the world looks at greatness is it?

The question is, how do you look at greatness?

Does this type of thinking go against how you look at things or support it?

It really begs the question, what is God's purpose for us?

Floodgates
by Rob Link

Have you ever fallen off the wagon?

I'm not necessarily talking about alcohol here – although that certainly could apply.

Rather I'm talking about getting away from good and right habits that you know are healthy and beneficial for you. It seems like I often have to battle against the lethargy that says, "Skip your devotional time today," "No need to take care of your body today; skip the gym," " Go ahead, be lazy, just this once." The problem is that when I give into these thoughts once, they have a way of forcing themselves on me again and again.

Once we open the door to compromise we might as well open the floodgates.

Where have you opened the floodgates of compromise?

How might you shut them?

Remember this is all under grace not shame.

Truth

by Brent Resh

The Lord detests lying lips, but he delights in people who are trustworthy.
Proverbs 12:22

One of the great things about God is that the things he wants us to do are for our own good.

You know how you feel after you tell a lie? It's not a good feeling.

You know what you've done isn't right and you wish you hadn't done it. Plus, you either have to come clean and tell the truth or continue to lie to cover your tracks and continue to have that rotten feeling inside.

That's why in the Bible God tells us over and over again the importance of being truthful.

God knows that when we always tell the truth, life is much easier for us. We don't have the weight of lies dragging us down.

Sometimes, though, it feels like it will be easier or better for us if we just lie about something.

We lie about lots of different things.

Maybe we didn't do what we said we would do, maybe we did something wrong and don't want to be caught, or we want people to think a certain way about us, so we make things up. Whatever it is we lie about, it seems like it's the best way out at the time. But once the lie is told, the work of covering up the truth begins.

We actually create work when we lie!

Mark Twain, the man who wrote the stories about Tom Sawyer and Huckleberry Finn, once said, "If you always tell the truth, you never have to remember anything."

How true!

When we lie, we have to try to remember all the things we made up. And the problem often becomes that once you tell a lie, you have to tell another and another and another so that you don't get caught in the first lie.

That's a lot to remember!

Sometimes we have to train ourselves to do what's right and prepare for things that will tempt us to do wrong. Usually when we lie, we ignore the feeling inside of us that's telling us to be truthful right before the lie is told. Train yourself to immediately tell the truth so that you take away the temptation to lie. You'll please God and find that you feel better about yourself too.

Has telling the truth been hard for you?

Is it hard for you to tell the truth now?

God wants to free you from that! If you desire to always be truthful, pray about it now. God will help you overcome it!

Running
by Rob Link

As I've aged and as my basketball injuries have mounted, I realized I needed a new hobby/exercise that wasn't so rough on my achy knees. Three ACL surgeries and numerous broken ankles, make the stop and go of hoops less than enjoyable.

So a number of years ago I took up running – very slow, low impact running.

There are quite a few parallels between running and the faith journey we call Christianity.

One time I was logging nine miles in preparation for a 15-miler my son Jake and I were running in.

At about Mile Six I realized I was having one of the best runs I've ever had.

It certainly wasn't because I was fast – I'm not. I'm quite slow actually.

I was having the run of my life because I found myself

living in the moment.

This was unusual for me when I ran. Up to that point in my running career, I usually spent the run thinking of how many more miles I had to go and getting bogged down with the weight of the future.

When I would focus on the future I would get stuck mentally and never enjoy the run.

But on that night I didn't have a thought for what was to come. I was simply living in the moment, and I was loving it.

Same is true for life. The responsibilities and fears of tomorrow can ruin our today if we let them. Jesus tells us in Matthew 6 to not worry about tomorrow.

So don't.

Don't worry about tomorrow. Be present in your "today."

You just might find that today is more enjoyable when you leave tomorrow alone.

How do you live life like I used to run?

How can you live more in the moment?

Good Dog/Bad Dog
by Rob Link

If you've ever been to church and seen Barkly greeting, you know how well behaved he is. When I say, "Sit," he sits. When I say, "Down," he lies down. While walking he will obediently stay right by my left leg when I say, "Heel." When I whistle he comes running. His obedience is very noteworthy.

And then there was that one Sunday afternoon. It was a different story that day.

I was upstairs reading when Reesah came running in to my room and said, "Dad, come quick Barkly is playing to rough with Max and isn't listening to anyone." As I ran out to the backyard I saw Barkly jumping up on Max and thoroughly ignoring any command Max gave him. Compared to his usual behavior it was as if he was an entirely different dog.

As I think of Barkly's drastically conflicting behaviors I am reminded of what the Apostle Paul said in Romans 7. In that chapter he talks about his own duality. One day walking in obedience to the master, the next day walking in sin. In verse 23 he says that there is a war being waged within. A war between his spirits desire to please God and his sinful desire to please the flesh.

Amidst this struggle he laments, "What a wretched man I am!"

Do you ever feel like Paul? Or Barkly? One moment committed to obedience and the next moment choosing disobedience. I think both Barkly's Sunday afternoon antics and Romans 7 epitomizes the plight of the human race.

Thank God (and I mean that – thank God!) for Romans chapter 8. In light of our goofy and ongoing duality it could be really easy to become discouraged and wonder how in the world could God love knuckleheads like us! Yet the end of the chapter brings peace to the conflicted and self-incriminating mind.

> *For I am convinced that neither death nor life, neither angels nor demons, neither the present nor the future, nor any powers, neither height nor depth, nor anything else in all creation, will be able to separate us from the love of God that is in Christ Jesus our Lord. Romans 8:38-39*

Nothing can separate us from the love of God. Nothing!

Not even our sinful disobedience.

This is good news.

In my "Barkly moments" I am prone to get really discouraged and to berate myself. These two verses remind me that God's grace has me covered even when I am at my worst.

So hear this, my friend – I still love Barkly a ton even though he was stupid that Sunday afternoon and God still loves you even in the midst of your own "Barkly moments."

When was your last "Barkly moment?"

How does it make you feel knowing God loves you in the midst of such times?

Mental Floss
by Rob Link

I only read one magazine regularly, and it's a good one.

Mental Floss.

It is a magazine for those who enjoy trivia, useless info, and weird facts. Each edition is chalked full of crazy information.

In one edition there was an article interviewing a laughologist. Yes that's right – a laughologist. This dude has dedicated 37 years of his life studying humans and laughing. (Who knew there was such a profession?!)

There was one thing in the article that was quite striking.

Babies laugh around 300 times a day on average. Usually deep, from-the-gut laughs.

Adults only laugh 20 times a day on average. Usually light, surface chuckles.

Great for the babies. Bummer for the adults.

As I read that I wondered, "What in the world takes place that robs adults of their laughter?"

Answer – life.

Life is difficult, as you know. We are assaulted from the moment we are born by things that work to steal our laugh. By the time we are grown, our laughter is greatly reduced.

> "...the joy of the Lord is your strength."
> Nehemiah 8:10
>
> ...you turned my wailing into dancing.
> Psalm 30:11
>
> "...there will be heard once more the sounds of joy and gladness..."
> Jeremiah 33:10-11

I think this decreased laughing is not of the Lord. He has Joy for us. The thief who comes to steal, kill and destroy (see John 10:10) has robbed us of our laughter.

I say no more!

Let's get our laugh back! Let's laugh like we did when we were babies.

Here's your assignment. Make laughing your work this week.

Chase things that you find funny, and laugh. Watch that old sitcom you used to laugh at. Read your favorite comic. Re-watch a funny movie.

Whatever it takes – laugh.

Laugh more.

Laugh often.

It's time we rescue our laughs!

Bonk.
by Rob Link

As I've been putting on some big miles running I've discovered this thing that folks in the runners world call "bonking."

Bonking is when you have depleted your energy reserves and are literally able to go no further.

I've found my very own anti-bonk potion.

It's called Gu.

Yes, I said Gu.

It was designed by runners for runners. It is a little packet of gooey stuff (hence the name you see) that is designed to be broken down quickly in your body and converted almost immediately to energy.

I love the vanilla bean Gu. Yummy. And energizing. (I must be honest that one person has described eating Gu is like having someone blow their nose in your mouth. That's kinda accurate in describing the texture.)

On my long runs I will intake a few Gu's. One every five miles. It is amazing the difference it makes.

Life is like running. Sometimes you just run out of energy and it feels like you just can't go one step further.

Fortunately God has given us something akin to Spiritual Gu.

The Bible tells us that we do not live by bread alone but by every word that proceeds from the mouth of God.

Could it be that God's Gu is the Word? I think so.

Just like I need some extra energy on my long runs, we all need something to make it through life without bonking.

When have you "bonked" in life?

What is your spiritual Gu?

Two Farmers
by Dan Smith

There had been a drought for weeks. Everything seemed to be hopeless for this year's crop. One farmer decided to pull back, to wait and see what would happen and gave up on continuing the process of preparing his field for harvest. Another farmer with the same dilemma kept on. He didn't give up on his field and continued his daily due diligence in preparing his field for harvest.   When the rain began to fall, who do you think trusted that God would bring the rain: the farmer who stopped and waited for rain before doing anything or the farmer who continued to prepare his field for the harvest?

> *Now faith is being sure of what we hope for and certain of what we do not see. This is what the ancients were commended for. By faith we understand that the universe was formed at God's command, so that what is seen was not made out of what was visible.*
> Hebrews 11:1-3

Does your faith in the Lord move you into action or are you waiting to be fully certain the Lord is moving first?

Have you ever felt like God had asked you to do something, not knowing what would happen if you did? How did you respond?

If you did respond, what did God do?

Where is He?
by Rob Link

A while back I spent fifteen days over in Israel walking the ground where our Bible took place.

It was an awesome experience.

We were able to sit where Abraham encountered God.

We walked the path the Israelites took while wandering in the wilderness.

We saw several places where Jesus walked.

To be in the places where it all happened was pretty doggone cool.

However, it was odd was to see countless people bow down and kiss a rock or touch a wall with tears in their eyes. In many places people apparently were struck with the urge to worship the place.

Weird.

Whereas I get the notion that it is pretty cool to see the "Holy Sites", I didn't get the urge to bow down and kiss a rock.

While I was pondering these things, I heard the still small voice of the Lord tell me, "I am as much in Kalamazoo as I was here in these so-called Holy Sites. I live with my people wherever they are. I am not stuck with a rock."

Now that's cool.

God is here with us.

Right here in Kalamazoo.

Or wherever you might be.

God is with us.

So for those of you who are bemoaning the fact that you can't get to the Holy Land, be of good cheer. You don't have to go there to encounter God's presence.

He is here.

With us.

With you.

Humility

by Rod Tucker

...your attitude should be the same as that of Christ Jesus:...
Philippians 2:5b

Wow!

This is quite the task. It is a good thing that the apostle Paul gives us more than just that verse alone.

Who, being in very nature God, did not consider equality with God something to be used to his own advantage, but made himself nothing by taking the very nature of a servant, being made in human likeness. And being found in appearance as a man, he humbled himself and became obedient to death – even death on a cross! Therefore God exalted him to the highest place and gave him the name that is above every name, that at the name of Jesus every knee should bow, in heaven and on earth and under the earth, and every tongue acknowledge that Jesus Christ is Lord, to the glory of God the Father.
Philippians 2:6-11

Christ was humble and obedient.

As a result of this, he was exalted to the highest place.

The reason God desires us to have the same attitude of Christ is so that we can also be exalted for his glory.

When we are humble we will be lifted up. When we are obedient we will be given more responsibility.

How's your humility level these days?

You Can
by Rob Link

I went backpacking a bit ago up in Canada with my son Zeke. He learned a couple things:

First, when attending to the necessary call of nature it is best to be about your business quickly. Otherwise the mosquitos will, um, how do I say this, create some interesting itching for you.

Second, Zeke is capable of more than he thinks he is.

And so are you.

You are capable of more than you think you are.

We were walking, loaded down with all the gear we would need for four days of backcountry camping, covering rocky terrain, going up and down, wearing head nets to keep the mosquitos at bay, sweating profusely when Zeke realized this trip with dad was more physically demanding than he had anticipated.

He shared his thoughts with me. This step of sharing a

struggle was huge. He could have suffered in silence and been miserable, but he knows his dad is there to help carry his burdens. When dad is around Zeke knows he isn't supposed to suffer in silence.

He knows he is to cast his cares upon his dad, because he knows his dad cares for him. (Sound familiar? Sound Biblical?)

As soon as he shared we stopped, sat down, and talked it through. I told him that we could stop right then and there, turn around and call it a trip. I told him there was no pressure to finish the trail. We could call it a day and head home. I also told him that I was sure he could do this. I was confident in him, his level of fitness, and his ability to overcome tough obstacles. I told him that if he decided to keep going I would be right there with him and that when it was all said and done he would feel really good about having overcome. I told him to take a few minutes and think it over.

He didn't need any time to process. He knew what he wanted to do.

He shouldered his pack and hit the trail.

We finished our three-night, four-day adventure. And Zeke

felt/feels awesome about having accomplished something he at first thought he wouldn't be able to do.

He learned that he is capable of more than he originally thought.

And so are you…

What tough things are you facing right now?

How close to quitting are you?

Finishing
by Rod Tucker

…being confident of this, that he who began a good work in you will carry it on to completion until the day of Christ Jesus.
Philippians 1:6

When God starts something he finishes it. When Jesus died on the cross for your sins and then three days later was raised from the dead, he did it all for you. If you do not have a relationship with Christ you can ask him to forgive your sins right now and come into your life.

If you do have a relationship with Christ, know that he will finish what he started in you. He has obligated himself to be your Heavenly Father, and that is always who he will be.

Nothing can separate you from God once he has adopted you as his child, and if you have asked to have a relationship with Christ you have been adopted as God's child.

Do you have a relationship with Jesus?

If not would you like to have one? Talk to your parents or a friend about this.

In > Out
by Rob Link

One of my sons plays varsity football. It had been a bit of a tough year. He hadn't been playing much.

Until week 6 of the season.

That week – he started.

And played very well. Several catches, a few of which were rather difficult. He was even able to add a few points to the scoreboard.

After the game, he was different than after the previous games. Sure he was bummed they lost yet he was pumped to have contributed in a significant way.

Pumped to have contributed in a significant way.

Being in the game sure does beat being out of the game.

Here's the parallel:

We were made to contribute significantly in this world.

We were made for impact.

Each of us has unique, God-given talents and abilities that we were given to make the world a better place.

Each of us.

You.

Me.

The difference is that there is no coach keeping us on the sideline. We get to play whenever we want to.

So get in the game. Make a difference.

Being in is better than being out.

What are your unique talents that you bring to the game called life?

If you are not in the game, what's keeping you on the sidelines?